INDOOR GARDENING

Hamlyn Practical Gardening Guides

INDOOR
GARDENING

Ann Bonar

HAMLYN

Published in 1989 by
The Hamlyn Publishing Group Limited
a division of the Octopus Publishing Group
Michelin House
81 Fulham Road
London SW3 6RB

© 1989 The Hamlyn Publishing Group Limited

ISBN 0 600 56484 3

Printed in Italy

CONTENTS

INTRODUCTION

The art of growing plants indoors has developed enormously from the original idea of having a few plants in terra-cotta pots, dotted about the house wherever there was a convenient space. There are now so many beautiful plants for the home, and so many new ideas for ways in which they can be grown and shown off, that the old hobby of collecting 'houseplants' has acquired a new term – 'indoor gardening'. Once you understand this, growing plants indoors becomes a new and fascinating art.

NEW IDEAS

Indoor gardening opens up all sorts of possibilities. To start with, it gets you away from plants grown just for their leaves – the picture once evoked by the word 'houseplant' – and suggests plants grown for their flowers, in addition to other plants such as climbers, annuals, bulbs, shrubs, herbs, and so on.

This new term suggests the continuous pleasurable process of gardening itself and its techniques – looking after, watering and feeding the plants, potting them on as they grow, and finally grooming and training them. It involves watching them

Indoor gardening suggests plants grown for their flowers, as well as those grown for their leaves.

7

unfold and expand day by day, as they come into flower, put out new shoots, develop miniatures of themselves, and set fruit and seed.

The great advantage of indoor gardening over outdoor cultivation, is that there are always plants in active growth, whether the season is winter or summer. You can have good flowering displays all year round, whereas the outdoor garden in winter will never be a patch on its appearance in summer, no matter how successfully you grow winter-flowering plants.

While you will not be able to plant the equivalent of herbaceous borders or beds full of carpet bedding, you can certainly get away from the one potted-plant-on-a-table syndrome, or one on the end of a shelf, with some magnificent displays. Part of the enjoyment of indoor gardening is experimenting with all sorts of ideas, and making use of household furnishings and equipment to enhance the plants – for instance, a mirror placed behind a plant gives a magical effect and creates the equivalent of a second plant. Such ideas

are tackled in more detail in the section on presentation and display.

Plants around the home
I haven't been rigid about the kinds of plants that should be grown in each room. It is often suggested that there are plants suitable for particular rooms – for instance bathrooms are considered particularly good for plants requiring humidity, and landings for shade-loving varieties, while living-rooms are thought to be appropriate for flowering plants, but in practice, such

Flowering begonias in the foreground and African violets in the background, bring colour to this mass of foliage plants.

A window position is ideal for light-loving plants, which bring life to stark spaces.

lose a few leaves annually – they don't retain all their leaves all their lives. Usually it is the oldest, low down on the stems, that turn yellow and drop first, mostly in spring when their new leaves are being produced.

Some foliage plants have plain green leaves, in interesting and dramatic shapes, or have attractive habits of growth. Others have 'coloured' leaves – that is, their leaves have additional colours besides green, or they are coloured like flowers, without any green at all. This may seem very peculiar, but in practice leaves and flowers are botanically not so very distinct.

In fact flower petals are modifications of leaves, and so are the green bracts out of which the petals emerge. The floral parts of stamens, stigma, and so on, are further developments from these, but sometimes the reverse happens, when petal-like stamens (staminoids) appear in the centre of the flower, coloured green, the stamens having reverted. To some extent also, 'coloured' leaves are the result of the light they receive in their natural habitat.

HERBS AND EXOTIC CHOICES

Growing plants indoors means that you can grow plants from much warmer climates than occur in Britain, and there is therefore a much wider range available for indoor gardening than there is for outdoors. All sorts of exotic varieties can be tried – with considerable success in many cases – such as the beautiful hibiscus of Pacific islands fame, the muskily scented four o'clock plant (*Mirabilis jalapa*) from Peru, and the majestic gloxinias, with their enormous velvety, trumpet-shaped flowers.

You will find that desert cacti thrive on sunny window-ledges. Also perfectly happy in the home are those extraordinary perching plants, the bromeliads, from South America, even though their natural resting places were once in the forks of giant tropical forest trees.

Indoor gardening suggests, too, that you can grow culinary plants, particularly herbs, in pots or troughs. Plenty of leaf is produced, often all the year round, to cut for flavouring by some, like thyme and winter savory, which are evergreen; others can be encouraged to grow for longer periods indoors, so that they can be used throughout most of the year.

generalizations don't always apply.

Certainly a bathroom may be humid, but it can also be very chilly, and consequently highly unsuitable for many plants which would have come originally from the warm tropical regions where there are monsoons. Nor are living-rooms always ideal for flowering plants, particularly if they are poorly lit. While some living-rooms may be continuously warm, they can have extremely dry atmospheres in winter, which few plants thrive in.

It is therefore much better to decide what kind of environment each room in your house can supply, and then choose your plants accordingly.

FLOWERS AND FOLIAGE

Another point well worth exploring is the seasons in which plants flower. So much research has been carried out by the container-plant suppliers into how to get plants to flower at different seasons to their normal ones, how flowering seasons can be extended, and whether there are plants which can bloom when few others do, that it is now possible to maintain a succession of flowering plants all the year round. Accordingly, in the section on flowering plants, I have divided the list into summer- and autumn-flowering plants, beginning on page 22, and winter- and spring-flowering plants, beginning on page 32, describing the varieties which flower during each period. Those plants which flower all the year round are listed on pages 40–42.

There are also alphabetical, descriptive lists of plants whose chief attraction is their foliage beginning on pages 43 and 55. Their growing season is mainly spring to mid autumn, but with the winter warmth of the home, many are likely to grow slowly through this season too. In any case, they are all evergreen and will be leafy throughout the year. However, don't forget that it is natural for evergreens to

The variegated ivy, *Hedera* 'Glacier' will trail elegantly over tables or shelves, softening harsh lines. *Pteris cretica* 'Alboliniata' adds height.

The indoor gardener is therefore presented with enormous variety. Gone are the days when plants were always only several centimetres high. You can now grow splendid specimens reaching to the ceiling, with the most spectacular results seen in the spacious, light entrances to modern office blocks. In fact, the plants found in such office blocks are an object lesson in what can be achieved with indoor gardening, both in the variety of plants grown and in the different, imaginative ways in which they are displayed.

Offices provide first-class homes for plants because of their large windows, and the higher the floor, the better the light. Modern houses echo this increased use of glass, whether through bigger windows, the glassed-in porch, or the lean-tos and conservatories attached to the home.

HOW IT ALL BEGAN

The cult of growing indoor plants really began with the Victorians, who enthusiastically scattered palms, aspidistras and ferns about the home.

Before the 19th century plants were

The maidenhair fern loves to be in a humid bathroom, as long as it is fairly warm.

rarely grown indoors – the light was very restricted, and warmth was by no means guaranteed in the average home during winter. It was mainly the wealthy, with their bright, warm homes, who successfully raised container-plants, and then mostly experimentally in the form of orange, lemon and fig trees in specially constructed, well-lit halls, many originally used for banquets.

However, the 19th-century Industrial Revolution radically altered everything, rather as the microchip is changing our present age, and coal fires in every room made the houses much warmer. Gas mantles provided more light in the evenings, and the removal of the tax on glass resulted in more and bigger windows.

The Victorians even had window gardens, like miniature greenhouses that extended out from the window, which were a good idea if you wanted to transform a blank wall. Other gardens consisted of glass cases inside the room; in addition to looking attractive, they had the advantage of protecting the plants from the 'fall-out' from the coal fires and the gas lights.

The Victorian Wardian case provided an environment for plants to flourish in, safe from gas-light and coal-fire fall-out.

Always take care to choose a pot that is compatible with the plant you intend to put in it.

PLANT PROBLEMS

Fortunately, oil-fired, natural gas, and electric central heating don't pollute the home or endanger the well-being of plants. In fact our biggest problem is probably dry air – lacking atmospheric moisture – caused by central heating, and made worse by the sealing effect of double glazing.

The only plants which can tolerate dry air are the desert cacti, the pelargoniums, most of the bromeliads, some of the palms, and a few other individual varieties. All the others need some degree of humidity to prevent their leaves turning brown at the edges and tips, or rapidly shrivelling up and falling. Without humidity, the flowers, too, fall quickly, and often buds drop before they have even opened. However, in Caring for Indoor Plants, page 80, I discuss methods of overcoming this problem. It is not difficult to provide humidity, and will be good for you as well as the plants.

Do note that falling leaves and flowers may well be indications of other troubles. If you find this is happening soon after you get the plants, it is quite likely to be due to the journey from the shop or garden centre, or that taken by your friend if the plant is a gift. Change of temperature, particularly if it drops on route, is the main culprit. Different lighting is another, and lack of water can also be a problem if you have not made sure that the plant is sufficiently moist when you receive it.

Plants for sale are usually in first-class condition; if they are not, and have yellowing leaves, are wilting, or have broken stems or branches, don't be tempted to buy them, even if the variety is outstandingly exotic or beautiful.

Look for a healthy plant, free from pests or diseases, such as greenfly or powdery

An eye-catching composition is formed by this group of plants.

white patches of mildew. Otherwise, the plant will have been weakened, treatment will be difficult, and in the meanwhile your other healthy plants may become infected and need treatment as well.

When plants which are ready for sale start to travel, the first journey from the wholesale nursery where they have been growing will be made quickly, in a custom-built van which will keep them stable and upright, and ensure protection from cold. Hence they are unlikely to be much affected by changes in environment while in transit at this stage.

During the journey from the florist's shop, nursery or garden centre, they will be exposed to quick changes in temperature, which may well be drastic, and also to draughts or wind. Although the plants will

be carefully wrapped by the assistant to protect them from these changes, a drop in the surrounding temperature is nearly always inevitable.

You can, however, make sure that draughts are not a problem, and if there is much wind, protection in a shopping-basket or all-enveloping carrier bag will help. Getting the plants home as quickly as possible will minimize the shock still more.

Once home, you should treat them as hospital cases, or at least as convalescents! Make sure the plants are securely anchored in their containers; have a look at the root-ball and, if it is well filled with roots, pot it on at once into a larger container with more, fresh compost. Otherwise leave it where it is, but water with tepid, soft water if the compost looks at all dry. Give the top growth a good misting with clear water.

Then put the plant in a warm place, slightly shaded, with a moist atmosphere. If humidity is difficult to provide, put a blown-up clear plastic bag over the whole of the top growth and secure it round the container rim. Leave it to settle down for a few days, and then move the plant to its permanent position.

Later in this book I will describe and give the cultivation details of over 150 plants. This is only a small proportion of the available range, with many of the more unusual varieties becoming increasingly available. Plant descriptions certainly are important, but it is the tips and hints for growing individual plants that make all the difference between a healthy and therefore ornamental plant, and a sick and ailing one. I hope that you will find this list helpful, and that you will have as much fun with growing plants indoors as I have.

DISPLAY AND DECORATION

Indoor gardening has one enormous advantage over outdoor gardening in that the plants are mobile. Outdoors, once you have planted the majority of them, they are permanent unless you are prepared to go to a great deal of trouble transplanting, possibly damaging and losing plants in the process.

Once indoors, the plants are self-contained. Since the root environment is portable, you can carry plants about and try them in various places in the house until you find the one where they both grow well and look their best. This is especially useful if you are not quite sure what kind of growing conditions they like. It may be that a plant needs more light than it is getting in the place where you first put it – for instance, one of the variegated ivies may be turning green – or you may find that it is growing so tall that it needs more space in preference to being cut back severely to the detriment of its appearance. The cane begonias are an example of such plants – they thrive in the home and rapidly grow one or two metres in height.

On the other hand, not every plant likes a lot of light, and the leaves of some can turn an unhappy shade of yellowish green. The grape ivy (*Cissus rhombifolia*) is one such plant – in sunlight or just bright light its foliage gradually loses its rich green colour until you begin to think it must be short of plant food.

ARRANGING PLANTS

The fact that you can move the plants about also means that you can experiment with combinations to obtain the most decorative groupings, which show the plants off to their best advantage. It may be a case of grouping together plants with different characteristics, so that you have a tall plant at the back, a couple of bushy varieties in front of it, and some trailers at their base.

Alternatively, it may be a case of blend-ing different coloured leaves or flowers, or both. You could have a lovely sunny arrangement of the yellow-variegated *Peperomia magnoliaefolia* 'Variegata', the devil's ivy (*Epipremnum aureum* 'Golden Queen') and one of the yellow varieties of the croton (codiaeum). Or you could select the royal purples – the stiffly twining purple heart (*Setcreasea purpurea*), the trailing hearts-entangled (*Ceropegia woodii*), *Zebrina pendula*, the wine-purple-leaved *Begonia rex* and the boat plant (*Rhoeo spathacea*).

If, accidentally, you have put two plants together which have different tastes – that is, one needs shade (for instance a green-

Mobility is the advantage of keeping plants in separate pots.

13

leaved ivy) and one requires sun (a desert cactus) – the problem can be solved readily. Sometimes a plant rapidly grows tall and dwarfs others in a group. For instance, the Swiss cheese plant (*Monstera*) initially can be quite small, then develops enormous leaves and quickly reaches a height of 2 m (6 ft), but, because it is portable, the difficulty is easily remedied.

Grouping plants in various ways like this is a natural development from the single-plant-in-a-pot idea. When plants started to appear in our homes, it was nearly always as one on a table, another on a bookcase and a third on the sideboard. Yet there is no reason why some should not still be grown as 'one-offs'. Indeed, some indoor plants are so magnificent that they deserve to be grown as specimens placed where they attract all the attention and become a focal point.

Alternatively, you can vary this style of display. Plants in collections make much more of a feature in a room, and they also grow better when close to one another because they all give off water-vapour so making the surrounding air much damper. It is also more natural for plants to grow close together – they are just as gregarious as human beings!

I have already suggested that plants in single pots should be grouped together. Now consider putting several plants in the same container. This certainly cuts down on chores such as watering, feeding and overhead spraying and also saves on compost. In addition, a flowering plant which is temporarily out of bloom can be disguised by attractive foliage plants.

Indoor gardens

A more ambitious extension of this idea is to devote a part of the floor of a room to creating a garden. This can be very successful, and with winter warmth can result in a miniature jungle! Extra lighting from spot lamps will encourage the plants to grow well, and there is no reason why you should not include a small pool in a suitable container. The smallest of the premoulded fibreglass pools for outdoors would do very well, and you could even add a fountain – small table fountains are widely available.

The main need with such an arrangement is to make absolutely certain that it is waterproof, and you could do this by first

Putting several plants in the same container cuts down on chores, such as watering, feeding and overhead spraying.

If creating a floor garden, make sure that the lining beneath it is really waterproof.

laying the heavy duty butyl rubber linings, used for pools and reservoirs, on the floor. Alternatively, you could use one of the shallowest formal square or rectangular fibreglass pools. But whatever you use, the watering must be very carefully done to avoid splashing the carpet or floor.

One vital point to remember when grouping plants, is that they should all have the same growing needs. I gave examples of this earlier in the chapter, discussing what can happen where different light needs clash. In addition, the plants should have similar temperature requirements in order to flourish.

The relevant details concerning growing requirements are supplied in the descriptive lists of plants on pages 22–79, but for the time being I list suggestions for different plant associations which you could try, using plants sold in small pots of about 5–6.5 cm (2–2½ in) in diameter. You can use bigger plants, of course, for an instant display, but watching the smaller ones grow and gradually fill up the spaces between to make the final picture is fascinating, and is part of the art and enjoyment of indoor gardening.

PLANTS THAT CAN BE GROUPED TOGETHER

1. Shrimp plant (*Beloperone guttata*) Australian silk oak (*Grevillea robusta*) Green ivy, small-leaved (*Hedera helix*) Aluminium plant (*Pilea cadierei*) Mother of thousands (*Saxifraga stolonifera*)	Good light MWT (minimum winter temperature) 10°C (50°F)
2. *Begonia rex*, varieties of Parlour palm (*Chamaedorea elegans*) Green ivy (*Hedera helix*)	Shade Moderate watering MWT 10°C (50°F)
3. *Peperomia magnoliaefolia* 'Variegata' Wandering Jew (*Tradescantia albiflora* 'Albovittata') *Codiaeum variegatum* – a yellow form Flame nettle (Coleus, yellow-variegated form)	Good light MWT 13°C (55°F)
4. Polka dot plant (*Hypoestes phyllostachya* 'Splash') Italian bellflower (*Campanula isophylla*) Persian violet (*Exacum affine*) *Begonia rex* 'Silver Queen'	Good light, a little occasional sun MWT 7.5°C (45°F)

5. Chrysanthemum – bronze or yellow-flowered *Kalanchoe blossfeldiana*, red or yellow-flowered Devil's ivy (*Epipremnum aureum* 'Golden Queen') *Pilea* 'Moon valley'	Good light MWT 10°C (50°F)
6. Hotwater plant (*Achimenes grandiflora*) Grape ivy (*Cissus rhombifolia* 'Ellen Danica') Swedish ivy (*Plectranthus oertendahlii*)	A little shade MWT 7.5°C (45°F)
7. Table or ribbon fern (*Pteris cretica* 'Albolineata') Hearts'-entangled (*Ceropegia woodii*) *Pilea* 'Norfolk' *Cyanotis somaliensis*	Good light MWT 10°C (50°F)
8. Goosefoot plant (*Syngonium podophyllum*) Wandering Jew (*Tradescantia fluminensis* 'Variegata') Ornamental or Christmas pepper (*Capsicum annuum*, yellow-fruited form)	Good light with occasional shade MWT 16°C (60°F)

UNDER THE SPOTLIGHT

In complete contrast, there are a good many indoor plants which can be given the spotlight and displayed as individual specimens. They are more than capable of holding their own, and attract attention because of their size, habit of growth, and perhaps even the unusual shape of their leaves. Often they have such dominating personalities that they will not fit into a

The Boston fern's cascading greenery makes it a celebrity among plants.

collection, because the other plants in it will be so forced into the background that they might as well not have been chosen.

The Boston fern (*Nephrolepis exaltata* 'Bostoniensis') is an example of an outstanding plant – it not only grows very fast, but it becomes large, and by the end of one year can easily be 60 cm (2 ft) in diameter.

The fronds arch over and hang down all around it, so that it looks marvellous either in a pedestal container, or placed high up where it can form a cascade of greenery. But in a group of plants its distinctive growth would be lost, and half the beauty of its appearance destroyed.

The false aralia (*Dizygotheca elegantissima*) is another 'personality' plant – tall, dark bronzy green, and with narrow, elegantly cut leaves radiating out in tiers around the main stem. So too is fatshedera, the hybrid between ivy and fatsia, with its lobed, large, ivy-like leaves decorating gently climbing stems. The most architectural plant of all is the Swiss cheese plant, *Monstera deliciosa*, from the jungles of Mexico. Its enormous leaves, slashed at the margins and perforated in the centre, demand special lighting and a white background so that its shadows are fully dramatized; by no means can its size and shape be fitted into a group.

In a lot of ways an individual specimen plant will be easier to place and care for than are collections of lesser plants. Although it will probably be large and take up a good deal of space, you need only worry about watering or feeding one plant, which often seems to last longer than individual plants in a collection. The amount of moisture which is given off by the sheer quantity of foliage ensures adequate humidity for the plant.

The large size of specimen plants also means that you won't have any problems filling space, while they are also a splendid complement to normal furnishings, bringing a room to life far more than a bowl of cut flowers ever will. Specimen plants achieve this for far longer, too, so altogether there is a lot to be said for a handsome example which will add to your indoor garden, be it a camellia, a cane begonia, a palm, or an umbrella tree.

Plant divisions

Specimen plants can be used to indicate room divisions, perhaps between a dining and living area, or between a general living space and an extension.

In offices, as well as homes, specimen plants are more than welcome, since they soften the hard lines of desks, filing cabinets, word processing and computing equipment. They are ideal for delineating boundaries between office areas, and for providing a little privacy and relief from the pressures of office life, as well as introducing changes of colour and texture, without destroying the necessarily professional air of a working environment.

Indeed, plants in general are becoming indispensable in all kinds of work places – factories, offices, hospitals, schools, and so on. There is no reason why they should not be grown in such situations, and often they are stronger and more colourful than they

are in a home because the temperature is consistent and a few degrees higher, at about 21–24°C (70–75°F) all the year round. Furthermore, lavish use of plate glass in modern industrial buildings provides the light that plants need, and so ensures that they grow and mature to their best and most decorative.

CONTAINERS

But whether you practise indoor gardening at home or in an office, don't forget that the containers in which the plants are grown can also be extremely ornamental. Terra-cotta clay pots were the original choices for the greenhouses and lean-tos of the Victorians. However, the plastic pots of the mid-20th century, though practical and convenient, are hardly decorative. Fortunately, if you prefer using them (despite their unprepossessing appearance) there are all sorts of attractive coloured and moulded ceramic pot covers which you can use to disguise them.

Clay pots not only look good, but they are better for a good many plants, being cool, moist and 'aerated', unlike the plastic variety. Most garden centres are now

stocking them again, but if you still have difficulty in obtaining clay pots, you could always ask a local potter to throw a few. Also look for clay containers in different, interesting shapes – urns and pedestals, troughs, pans, and so on.

Even better are the kind with designs etched into the outside of the clay, or with swags and garlands of flowers, leaves, and all sorts of other decorations in relief. Also look out for colours other than terra-cotta; reconstituted stone can be coloured white, cream, or sandstone. Some are even coloured and moulded to look like the antique Italian containers, embossed with cherubs, fruit and cornucopias.

However, there is no reason why you should not use plastic containers, as an alternative. They are available in a wide range of colours, besides terra-cotta. And there is a particularly agreeable range with a matt surface and matching saucers in pleasantly muted shades of green, stone, and brown. If you want something bright to set off a green foliage plant, or to complement a flower colour, there are red, yellow and white plastic containers as well (white always looks good and boosts the appearance of any plant tremendously). A

An extensive range of ornamental containers is readily available.

deep chocolate brown can be unexpectedly attractive, enhancing the dignified and handsome appearance of specimen plants, in particular, without overwhelming them.

Another choice of material is wood, and there are some extremely attractive wooden tubs and troughs to be found, giving an even more natural appearance than clay. But if you still cannot find just the right container, it is quite possible to make one to your own design out of plastic-covered chipboard, especially if you want an unusual size for a group of plants, or you have ambitions to have the indoor garden referred to earlier.

Square or rectangular boxes attached to one another, some shallow and some deep, to take plants with different requirements and of different heights, will give you a display which is constantly changing as the plants grow. Waterproofing is again important, especially where the sections are joined.

The colour of the container will have to be chosen with care, however. You don't want the tail to wag the dog, and find that all your friends are congratulating you on the containers and not the plants!

If you are at all concerned with colour, there is the further point of matching plant and container, especially where flowers are concerned and where you are deliberately blending colours, whether of flowers or leaves. You may be combining shades of purple, pink and lavender, for instance, or associating plants with blues and yellows in their flowers and leaves; you may be seeking to create a silvery grey effect, or a dazzlingly golden one.

In outdoor gardening, colour is a primary consideration. It is one of the main reasons for growing ornamental garden plants, and there is no reason why it should not be one of the objectives in an indoor garden display, too. The huge range of plants suitable for the home or office allows you not only to focus on colours, but to integrate them with the colours of your furniture, wall and floor coverings and pictures. Each room can have plants complementing or contrasting with the colour scheme, so that you could, for example, have certain plants echoing the wallpaper design, others contrasting with the curtains, the rest reflecting the dominant colour in the carpet.

THE CLIMBERS

When selecting plants, don't only consider their colour but also their climbing potential. Climbing plants lend themselves to all sorts of places and arrangements.

The corners of a room are too easily forgotten – why not place a climbing plant at the bottom to fill up the area and highlight the meeting of the two walls. Use

An assortment of shallow and deep containers suits plants of different heights and requirements.

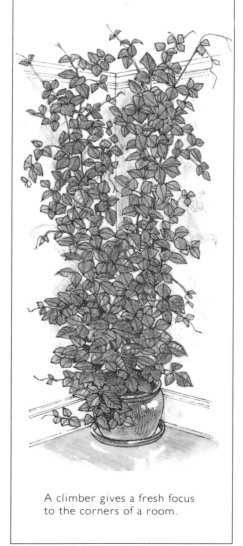

A climber gives a fresh focus to the corners of a room.

Consider decorating a window, door, mirror or picture with a plant frame by training climbers up the sides and across the top.

to a support using short aerial roots; and others produce tendrils which coil round the nearest stem, or cane in this case.

Depending on the vigour of the plant you will need one, two, or more canes. You can also use a plastic-covered trellis, specifically made for contained plants, which is stuck into the compost.

If the plant is a species which produces long aerial roots, a moss pole is the answer. The damp moss will allow the roots to absorb moisture, and the whole plant will grow better as a result.

In addition to the natural climbers, there are some upright and stiffly growing plants that can be trained into various shapes and coaxed to act like climbers. The pelargonium with lemon-scented and yellow-variegated leaves is one which responds very well, and can be trained into circular, triangular, pyramidal or ball silhouettes. So, too, can any small climber, such as the small-leaved ivies, black-eyed Susan (*Thunbergia alata*), and the creeping fig (*Ficus pumila*).

Although climbing plants can often provide a spectacular part of an indoor plant display, do not forget that other forms also have much to offer. There are rounded bushy plants, and upright varieties, reminiscent of miniature trees; there are also low-growing kinds, and arching plants. Some have large, impressive leaves, others are delicate and graceful. Flowering may be profuse for a short period, or persistent for many weeks, though making less of a display. But whatever type of plant you select, the possibilities for combining it imaginatively with other plants, or setting it off against a feature or colour scheme in a room are endless.

tall canes with soft string trained up and round each cane for the stems to get a grip on, or you can use moss poles instead. Such poles are usually used for plants with aerial roots, but there is no reason why ordinary climbers should not be given them for support.

Growing decoration

Another attractive idea is to use a climber on each side of a mirror to provide a living frame, or you can use this effect around a picture. Continuing the idea, why not train climbers up the sides of a door, or use them to soften the edges of a window which has blinds instead of curtains? For really vigorous climbers, attach a panel of green diamond-shaped trellis to the wall and tie the plant's stems to this as they grow. But if you do use this arrangement, make sure you have a waterproof drip saucer for the container, and remember that because the plant is now a permanent fixture, repotting will be difficult.

You will need a tub for this kind of climber, but do ensure that such vigorous growers as white jasmine – which has strongly fragrant flowers all summer – have the appropriate size container. Too often jasmine is confined to a 13-cm (5-in)

diameter container, and cut back hard, never really being given a chance to display its ability to flower.

Some old houses have vertical wooden beams or pillars in the middle of a large room which may have been converted from two smaller rooms. Such structures are ideal for climbing plants, providing a ready-made support. Wide inglenook fireplaces can look good wreathed in leafy climbing plants on either side, and in some country houses hops, with their cone-like flowers, are used in this way. A sunny glassed-in porch could have Cape leadwort trained up the sides and along the underside of the roof or, less permanently, you could try nasturtiums.

Support

Climbers grown on their own to provide a vertical rather than a bushy shape can be held upright by several different supports. Canes are the most obvious kind to which the stems can be tied with soft string, or twist-ties. However, other climbers naturally grasp the canes. The sweetheart vine (*Philodendron scandens*) automatically twines its stems around the support; some climbers, such as the ivies and the wax flower (*Hoya carnosa*), attach themselves

On display

Mirrors will substantially increase the effect of a display, when placed behind it. Well-sited lighting can bring a plant to life (literally), but focused wrongly will ensure that it recedes into the background. Try comparing the results of spotlighting a specimen plant first from in front, then from above, from the side, from floor level, and from behind. In each case, the different qualities in the plant will be emphasized, and, importantly, it can be made to look more interesting than it actually is.

Backgrounds, too, are significant. They

A spider plant in a macramé hanging basket disguises an ugly angle.

Tradescantia 'Quick Silver' is an ideal trailing plant.

A hanging basket suits the pendulous begonias.

The Italian bellflower *Campanula isophylla*, flowers profusely.

can make or break a display, so you should take them into account when deciding what plants to use, and where to put a group. Patterned wallpapers are often too busy and distracting, and can overwhelm some plant groups, but an arrangement of foliage plants in various shades of green could be highlighted by such a wallpaper. A white background will usually focus attention on the plants, while plain coloured walls can form part of the colour-scheme of a plant display.

Plants in space

So far I have been talking about objects and the ways in which they can affect the appearance of a display, but what about space? How can that be used to set off your plants to their best advantage?

Plants placed on the floor, or on furniture, or on stands, obviously become focal points. But what might be defined as aerial space – that in which plants hang – is quite different. In order to fill this kind of space you will need the trailing plants such as the

Flowering and glossy-leaved trailing plants are very attractive aerial space-fillers.

For trouble-free watering of hanging plants, use a pump-can with a long spout to reach into the baskets.

Italian bellflower (*Campanula isophylla*), hearts-entangled (ceropegia), species of tillandsia (the bromeliad air plants), pendulous begonias, tradescantia, zebrina, and so on.

You should also consider the plants with long stems ending in plantlets – such as the spider plant (chlorophytum) and the mother-of-thousands (*Saxifraga stolonifera*). Another possibility involves encouraging the smaller climbers, for instance, ivies, nasturtiums, the devil's ivy (*Epipremnum aureum*), and black-eyed Susan (*Thunbergia alata*), to trail. Creeping plants will also trail over the sides of hanging containers and down into the air – some of the best plants to chose are the creeping fig (*Ficus pumila*), the Swedish ivies (plectranthus), and the snakeskin plant (fittonia).

Containers for growing such plants include hanging baskets, pots in macramé hangers, and pots with plastic hangers clipped to the rims. Baskets have come a long way from the originals made of a wire framework, and are now, inevitably, made of plastic, either forming a complete sheet, or being slatted. Some have drip saucers as an integral part of the basket; some can be lined with compressed peat, so avoiding the use of sphagnum moss; and some are made of recycled cellulose (paper!) dyed and formed into a hanging basket shape into which the plants can root, and which sometimes have nutrients incorporated.

Macramé hangers are available with different thicknesses of string, cord or rope, and are knotted in a variety of eye-catching ways. They are also lightweight and inexpensive. Drip saucers can easily be fitted at the base. Lighter still are the plastic pots with an attached saucer and plastic 'strings' which are fastened to the rim of the pot by small clips. They are ideal for small plants and are surprisingly effective for aerial display.

Watering plants which are hanging at head height can be a problem, but the new pump-cans overcome such difficulties. They have long spouts which reach into the containers, making it unnecessary to lower them.

Aerial-space plants can be hung against walls, too, either in half baskets made of clay with a flat back, or in wall hangers of white or black wrought iron, designed to hold pots of varying sizes. This is quite an

Busy Lizzie (*Impatiens*) produces vibrantly-coloured flowers all the year round.

A raft suits trailing orchids and the stag's horn fern.

ingenious way of filling blank wall space without having to use climbing plants and the necessary supports, and it doesn't necessarily restrict you to trailers – the smaller bushy or upright plants will be just as good.

Another way of using aerial space involves free-standing vertical plant supports made of bamboo, metal, or plastic. Some have rings on arms, spaced at intervals, up the central pole; some have cups on arms; and some are 'tower blocks' which contain compost into which the plants are put directly, and which rule out the need for separate pots.

'Trees' made of dead branches fixed upright look good with bromeliads planted in peat at the junctions of side branches, and will provide particularly good homes for air plants (tillandsia species). Small hanging wooden platforms, or large pieces of cork bark with fibrous peat bound on to them, will suit the stag's-horn fern and some of the orchids.

In fact the more you think about aerial space, where you can look at plants at or above eye-level, the more you will think up striking new ways of displaying indoor plants. The more imaginative your ideas, the more attractive and spectacular the plants will become.

PLANTS FOR SUMMER AND AUTUMN FLOWERING

This chapter deals with indoor plants which flower in the summer and autumn. In the alphabetical section which follows, details of the plants are given; they are referred to first by their botanic name, and then by the common name, if there is one. If you only know the common name of a plant, the quickest way to track it down will be to consult the index.

Although the listing of plants in this and in the following chapter is based on the seasons, do note that many plants which start to bloom in summer go on flowering well into autumn, some even into early winter. Amongst those which start in spring are two that continue into summer: *pachystachys* and *spathiphyllum*. This is one of the joys of indoor gardening; you can actually have a much greater collection of flowering plants indoors in winter than will be outdoors, when most plants have put up a massive defence against the cold, and have either retired beneath the soil completely or shed their most vulnerable parts.

MWT = minimum winter temperature.

Achimenes (hot-water plant)

These pretty little plants (originally from Mexico) are bushy or trailing, and are profusely covered in trumpet-shaped flowers mostly in shades of blue, violet or pink, although less common hybrids can be yellow, red, white or orange. The flowering starts in early summer and continues well into autumn with a succession of flowers. The plant's height is about 20–25 cm (8–10 in). The name is thought to derive from an old belief that the water supplied to the plants should be hot.

Easily grown, they are happy with average humidity, moderate watering, a good light and ordinary summer temperatures. In winter, the small tuber-like rhizomes should be left in their containers and kept at 7.5°C (45°F) or above; in early spring discard the smallest, and plant the remainder 13 mm (½ in) below the compost surface, putting two in a 10-cm (4-in) diameter pot of peat-based compost. Provide split canes for support and a starting temperature of at least 16°C (60°F).

Bouvardia domestica

Evergreen and bushy, growing about 60 cm (2 ft) tall in three or four years, this plant from South America flowers from mid summer into early winter. At the end of the shoots there are clusters of pink, red or white, scented tubular flowers.

The plants are not difficult to grow, and were once used for outdoor bedding plants. Now *Bouvardia domestica* makes an excellent pot plant for the home.

The main requirement is to pinch back the shoots frequently to make the plants bushy, and encourage them to flower well, otherwise they become leggy, with few flowers. A good light is essential, but not bright sun, together with average humidity, plenty of water while growing, and a minimum winter temperature of 10°C (50°F), when they should be kept nearly dry. Cut them back hard in late winter and start into growth again with increased watering and a raised temperature.

Browallia speciosa (bush violet)

Although a member of the same family as the tomato, this summer-flowering annual plant has quite a different flower shape. The five flat, open petals are attached to a tube, and look much more like those of the aubergine, also in the same family. The colour is blue-purple, and the flowers can cover the plant all summer and autumn; there are white, and white-edged varieties. The bush violet's place of origin is South America.

Remove the tips of shoots (see page 83 for technique) to retain a compact and prolifically flowering plant.

The trailing Italian bellflower's great popularity as a houseplant is partly due to the ease with which it is grown.

Plenty of water, a good light with some sun, and average humidity will suit it best, as will a summer temperature of 10–16°C (50–60°F). Remove the tips of shoots to keep the plants compact and to encourage them to flower well. Liquid feeding will be necessary.

Campanula isophylla (Italian bell-flower)

This is one of the easiest plants to grow indoors; it starts to flower in mid summer and continues until mid autumn, if not longer. A trailing plant about 30–38 cm (12–15 in) long, it has blue or white open bell-shaped flowers 4.5–5 cm ($1\frac{3}{4}$–2 in) wide covering the stems, and not surprisingly, considering its common name, it comes from Italy.

New shoots appear in the autumn, which will flower the following year. Cut off the old flowered shoots when flowering finishes, and keep the compost just moist; MWT 7.5°C (45°F); repot in early spring. During the summer, provide plenty of water, average humidity and temperatures, and a good light.

Capsicum annuum (Christmas pepper, ornamental pepper)

The ornamental peppers are related to the larger sweet peppers and those from which cayenne and paprika are made. They owe their decorative qualities to their small, brilliantly coloured fruit in orange, red, yellow and purple, which are preceded by white flowers in summer. Some hybrids bear their fruit in summer as well. They remain colourful for many weeks, but are then discarded.

The pointed fruits are edible but unpleasantly hot and should not be used in cooking. The plants originate from tropical America.

Provide a good light, including sun, plenty of water, frequent overhead spraying (otherwise the fruit drops), and MWT of 13°C (55°F).

Christmas pepper, *Capsicum annuum*'s common name, is a misnomer for the hybrids which bear their glowing fruits in summer as well as winter.

The flame violet's scarlet flowers contrast startlingly with its dark green and silver foliage.

Episcia cupreata (flame violet)

A pretty little ground-covering plant which can be allowed to trail over the container side. It has attractive, dark green, wrinkled foliage banded in the centre, with pale green or silver, and contrasting bright vermilion tubular flowers in summer. The stems root at the leaf-joints to provide new plantlets. The flame violet is a native of South America.

Episcias must have constant high humidity – and therefore grow well in groups. Regular overhead misting is also necessary for them to flourish. They also require a good light and should be kept in constantly moist, but not waterlogged compost. The MWT should be 13°C (55°F) with moderate watering.

Fragrance is a special feature of the Persian violet, which will bloom until mid autumn, as long as dead flowers are removed regularly.

Exacum affine (Persian violet)

Like the ornamental peppers, this is a 'throwaway' plant, grown from seed each year, sown under glass in 18°C (65°F) in late winter. By early summer it will start to produce its small but plentiful fragrant purple flowers with yellow centres, covering a small bushy plant about 18 cm (7 in) tall and wide. Blooming continues until mid autumn, provided dead flowers are removed regularly. The plant is a native of the island of Socotra, in the Indian Ocean.

A good light, and ordinary summer temperatures suit it. Average watering and good humidity are also required.

Fuchsia

Among the easiest and most ornamental of plants to grow, fuchsias do particularly well in containers. Their distinctive dangling flowers first appear in mid summer and, in the right conditions, can continue until well into the winter, if not the following spring.

There are many hybrids with flowers coloured in various combinations of purple, pink, white, magenta, red, blue-purple, and in all shades of these colours. A typical fuchsia flower has red outer petals and purple inner ones. Some are single – the prettiest are double, and these need the most care.

Fuchsias can be grown as small bushy shrubs, standards, and trailing plants; some can be trained into an interesting variety of shapes including balls, triangles and pyramids. Whether specially trained or not, pinched-back shoots in late spring will ensure more flowers. Turn to pages 82–3 for an illustrated description of the pinching-back technique.

Provide plenty of water while growing and flowering, and a good light but not direct sun. Provide overhead misting on a regular basis, applying it particularly to the stems and main trunk. Ensure that the MWT is 4.5°C (40°F) and the summer temperature is below 24°C (75°F).

You should also keep the compost barely moist in winter, when the leaves drop, and prune in late winter by cutting last year's new growth back by half. Bud and flower drop can be a problem if air and/or compost are dry, or the temperature is too high. Watch for whitefly and red spider mite.

Hibiscus rosa-sinensis (Chinese rose)
The Chinese rose is one of the more exotic plants that can be grown in the house. It is a shrubby, evergreen plant that can grow to about 60–90 cm (2–3 ft) tall, and 60 cm (2 ft) or more wide.

The large trumpet-shaped, single or double flowers, with their prominent central column carrying the stamens, are usually in shades of pink, red or white, though yellow, orange and salmon hybrids are available. The variety *cooperi* has leaves variegated cream and deep pink, with rose-pink flowers. The plant originates from China.

A good light, plenty of water, and warmth and humidity are required during the growing and flowering period. Reduce the watering to keep the compost just moist in winter, so maintaining the leaves but not encouraging growth. Also supply a MWT of 13°C (55°F), and prune, either immediately after flowering or in late winter by cutting last year's new growth back by a half to two-thirds.

Red spider mite and scale insect can be problems. Information on eradicating them is given in the chapter on Caring for Indoor Plants, which begins on page 80.

Hoya carnosa (wax flower)
Queensland, Australia is the home of this vigorous evergreen climber, which can easily grow 1.8 m (6 ft) in a season.

In early summer, stiff clusters of pale pink, star-like flowers appear, each with a drop of sweet, sticky liquid exuding from the centre. In the evening the flowers' fragrance becomes very strong. In the right conditions, flowering can continue until autumn.

A good light is important for flowering (but not direct sun), average humidity (more when in flower), average watering and normal summer temperatures, and a MWT of 10°C (50°F).

Use plant supports, preferably moss sticks, so that the aerial roots on the stems can attach themselves. For additional interest, consider training the plant into one of a variety of shapes. For instance, a triangle makes an especially eye-catching choice.

If pruning is required to keep the plant within the space available, do this in late winter. Do not remove the flower stalks, as some of next year's flower buds will come from their base. Repot the plant only when pot-bound.

Some fuchsias can be trained into decorative shapes, such as triangles and pyramids.

Hypocyrta glabra (clog plant)

Many of the plants in this family make good subjects for indoor gardening and the clog plant is no exception. Small and bushy, it grows to 23 or 25 cm (9 or 10 in) tall with the same spread.

The evergreen leaves are thick, shiny and dark green, making an attractive display even when the plant is not blooming; the 2.5-cm (1-in)-long flowers are orange, later turning red. Intriguingly pouch-like in shape they appear between early and late summer. The plant is a native of Brazil.

Give the clog plant a good light, but not sun, moderate watering as its fleshy leaves can store water, and good humidity. Mist the leaves regularly. Normal summer temperatures and a MWT of 10°C (50°F) suit the clog plant. Prune in late winter or early spring by cutting the stems back by one third of their length.

Jacobinia carnea

The jacobinias were once commonly grown in warm greenhouses, and only recently have become fashionable indoors where they flower in late summer-early autumn. Clusters of bright pink, tubular flowers unfold at the end of shoots on a bushy evergreen plant, which can in time be 1.2 m (4 ft) tall, and nearly as wide. It comes from Brazil.

A good light and plenty of humidity are important. Water well in summer, very moderately in winter, and keep at average temperatures in summer with a MWT of 13°C (55°F). Feed in summer and repot in spring in alternate years.

Jasminum (jasmine)

The summer-flowering jasmine, *Jasminum officinale grandiflora*, comes from eastern Asia; it is hardy enough to be grown outdoors in sheltered gardens, but indoor growing will ensure that the plant is not killed by frost.

The strongly fragrant small white tubular flowers are produced profusely and successively from early summer until early autumn, often longer, on vigorously twining stems which can reach 6 m (20 ft). Several canes will be needed to support one plant.

Pruning is done after flowering – cut back the shoots which have flowered by about half their length, and cut new ones to fit the space available. While growing in summer, tie the shoots to the canes to prevent them from becoming tangled, and thin out crowded ones.

Plenty of light and water, with normal summer temperatures and humidity, and a MWT of 7.5°C (45°F) will suit the jasmine. Feed it with a potash-high liquid fertilizer from mid summer onwards to maintain the strong growth.

Jasmine will reward summer attention and autumn pruning by flowering abundantly and fragrantly throughout the summer.

Bright, glass-like berries jostle with one another to conceal the tiny leaves on the aptly named bead plant.

Musa (banana)

The banana plant is native to tropical parts of the world, and needs high temperatures. The one whose varieties supply the common fruit is *M. paradisiaca sapientum*, growing to 7.5 metres (25 ft), with leaves 2.4 metres (8 ft) long and 60 cm (2 ft) wide!

But there are two small species suited to indoor growing: *M. coccinea* and *M. velutina*. The former is the red banana, whose red flowers appear in summer on a plant about 90 cm (3 ft) tall, followed by tiny bananas, only about 5 cm (2 in) long, and not really edible. *M. velutina* is a little taller, reaching a height of about 1.2 m (4 ft), with yellow flowers in summer, and bright red, small, velvety fruits, which are also inedible.

Fruiting is unlikely in the home, but both species make interesting foliage plants which will flower, with careful cultivation. Pot into successively larger pots to a final size of 25 cm (10 in) diameter; use a soil-based compost, and give a good light with some sun every day whenever possible, particularly in winter. MWT should be 18°C (64°F), much higher from spring to autumn, when they should be watered copiously as they will grow very fast. Mist the leaves frequently; a very humid atmosphere is vital. In winter, water moderately to sparingly, and reduce the humidity also as too much moisture can result in the roots rotting.

Nertera depressa (bead plant)

An intriguing little plant which grows in mats along the surface of the soil. The small round leaves are almost hidden by bright orange, round berries the size of a pea, which follow the greenish, tiny flowers, and last through summer into autumn. The plant originates from Australia, New Zealand and South America.

Average summer temperatures and reasonable humidity suit it. While flowering and fruiting it needs a good light with some sun and plenty of water, but in winter the compost should be barely moist. It is easily increased by separating chunks of rooted stems in spring and potting in peat-based compost. The MWT should be about 4.5°C (40°F).

Oliveranthus harmsii (syn. *Echeveria harmsii, Cotyledon elegans*)

A pretty, summer-flowering succulent plant uncommon for this group of plants, which are usually grown for the sake of their fleshy leaves. Oliveranthus has trailing stems up to 45 cm (18 in) long, carrying inflated, tube-like flowers about 2.5 cm (1 in) long, coloured red with yellow tips, during mid and late summer. The leaves are mostly gathered into rosettes, and this leaf formation is typical of many succulents. A native of Mexico.

Pot only when the soil-ball is really full of roots, and use a half pot, or a similar shallow container, when repotting in spring. Supply a MWT of 7.5°C (45°F), and water very sparingly in winter, at intervals of four to six weeks. In summer, water like a normal plant, provide plenty of light with sun – this is essential – and don't worry about humidity. If the plant gets straggly, cut the stems back after they have flowered, to keep it bushy.

Pelargonium (geranium)

The pelargoniums are a marvellous family of plants for indoor gardening – they are easily grown, flower profusely (some almost all year round), and are almost indestructible. The plants are very strong and can withstand a great deal of maltreatment and neglect. Varieties come in all sizes, large or small, upright, bushy or trailing; the flowers are in all shades of scarlet, pink, red, orange, magenta, salmon, crimson verging on black, and white; the leaves can be variously coloured, as well as plain green. Some varieties have heavily aromatic leaves. Most come from South Africa.

The zonal pelargoniums are the ones usually known as geraniums, with ball-like heads of flat, five-petalled flowers, and a dark brownish band on the upper surface of each leaf. Colours are mostly in the red, pink or white range; flowering will start in early summer and continue until late autumn. In fact, flowering all through winter is not unknown, but it is better to discourage this tendency, and to induce a resting period by lowering the temperature to about 7.5°C (45°F) and keeping the compost almost dry. Height is about 30–45 cm (12–18 in), though pelargoniums can be trained flat against a wall to grow many feet tall in a frostproof conservatory.

Regal hybrids have four or five trumpet-shaped flowers with frilly margins in a cluster, which last for a few weeks only, through mid and late summer. Each flower is about 4–5 cm (1½–2 in) wide, and colours are much more varied, through shades of orange, pink, red, magenta and crimson to almost black.

Miniature hybrids are about 15 cm (6 in) tall, often with leaves coloured in reds and yellows, and have the geranium type of flower. Trailing varieties have ivy-shaped leaves, being white-veined on green ('Crocodile'), or white-edged and flushed pink on grey-green ('L'Elegante'), which also has very pretty white flowers.

Geraniums are among the great survivors of the houseplant world, responding to neglect and mistreatment by flowering almost non-stop.

Those with aromatic leaves have small narrow-petalled flowers, and leaf fragrances of lemon, rose, balsam, eucalyptus, apple, and so on, but all other pelargonium varieties have leaves with a different aroma, peculiar to the genus.

Their main requirement is a good sunny light, which is essential; water well, but allow the compost to dry between waterings, and water sparingly in winter. Normal summer temperatures will suit them; supply a MWT of 7.5°C (45°F) – the trailing kinds of pelargonium need a MWT of 10°C (50°F). Humidity is not a requirement.

Prune by pinching out the tips of regal and zonal shoots in spring to keep the plant bushy; this method is described on page 83, in the chapter on Caring for Indoor Plants. Cut back the summer's growth in autumn to leave about 10–13 cm (4–5 in) of growth. Other kinds can be cut back to keep them from becoming leggy, if this seems likely. Remove the flowerheads as they fade.

Plumbago capensis (Cape leadwort)
This is another plant from South Africa, but of quite a different growth habit and colouring to the pelargoniums.

The Cape leadwort is a strong climber which needs a large pot or small tub to contain its vigorous root-ball. It can be trained to frame a specific object – a window or conservatory door, for instance. Growth can easily be many centimetres (several feet) a year. In summer light blue flowers, 2.5 cm (1 in) wide, appear in many-flowered clusters, and flowering will continue well into the autumn.

The Cape leadwort needs good sunlight to ensure satisfactory flowering, average watering, humidity, and summer warmth. In winter it needs to be cool, but in a temperature not less than 7.5°C (45°F), and kept on the dry side. Prune the plant hard immediately after flowering has finished to encourage good new shoot production the following spring, on which the next season's flowers will appear.

Rochea coccinea (crassula)
There are lots of plants whose botanical name is Crassula, but the common name of this one refers to a plant with quite a different botanical name, so if you want this particular species, it is best to ask for it by the botanical name given above.

This is the only rochea grown as a pot plant at present, and it makes a pretty specimen. The small, star-shaped flowers consist of a tube with the petals attached to it, coloured rosy red, in a cluster at the top of a stem about 38 cm (15 in) tall. Each plant has several of these stems, from which small, succulent, triangular leaves project horizontally in fours all the way up the stem, giving the plant a very formal appearance, almost like a model of a plant.

From South Africa, the MWT should be 4.5°C (40°F); watering should be sparing in winter but in summer normal temperatures and watering are required, together with a good light and some sun. Humidity is not essential; repot in spring.

Saintpaulia ionantha (African violet)
You could easily fill the house with African violet hybrids and not repeat any of them, so many are the variations on the original purple, yellow-centred species. Colours now include various shades of blue, pink, wine, and red, as well as purple, lilac, lavender, and white. Some are two-coloured, edged or striped; some are double-flowered; and some are fringed or ruffled. A few have variegated leaves.

There are miniature forms of African violet in varying degrees of smallness, and 'trailing' kinds, which form plantlets at the end of stems. Many named hybrids are available. The plant's place of origin is central Africa.

Flowering can continue for most of the year, but not continuously, usually in four or five flushes, with a rest in mid to late winter. Plenty of humidity is vital, since it is possible that moisture is absorbed through the thick furry leaves.

Give a steady temperature of normal warmth in summer, and a MWT of 16°C (60°F); water carefully when the compost surface is dry, but do not over-water and avoid splashing the leaves. Supply a good light but not sun, and light in the evening for winter flowering.

Use peat-based compost and a plastic half-pot (pan), and only pot when the plant begins to be crowded. Remove offsets from the base as soon as they form, and plant them up, when they will quickly make small new plants.

Sinningia (Gloxinia)
Together with the double-flowered begonias, the gloxinias (which come from Brazil) are the most handsome of the flowering plants for indoor gardening. Most of those grown now are the result of hybridizing, and there are many beautiful named varieties.

The rather fleshy flowers are large, bell-shaped, about 10 cm (4 in) long and 6.5 cm (2½ in) wide, with a velvety appearance and feel. Colours are in the range of crimson, purple, pink, red and blue. Some are bicoloured, with a white edging, or with spots and veining on a white background (the latter are called the Tiger hybrids).

They need a good deal of space, because the leaves can be 20 cm (8 in) long and

The gloxinia's opulent blooms have a velvety texture that tempts you to stroke them.

nearly as wide, and one plant can have at least 20 flowers on it. Flowering is from mid summer to autumn.

Gloxinias grow from a tuber, and while growing need a good light, but not sun, and average summer temperatures – above 27°C (80°F) they begin to wilt. Water freely in summer and provide humidity. In winter supply a MWT of 10°C (50°F) and keep completely dry; in spring repot the tuber just below the surface of new, moist compost, keeping the hollow side facing upwards. Keep warm, and water only when the growth is well under way.

Solanum capsicastrum (Christmas cherry, Jerusalem cherry)

This is a bushy little plant grown for its bright and cheerful, orange-red, marble-sized berries which cover a 30-cm (12-in) tall plant in autumn and winter. They are preceded by white flowers in summer.

There is a form with white-splashed leaves, and another with scarlet fruits, and all can remain colourful for many weeks. They are available from autumn onwards, but are usually discarded once the leaves start to change colour and fall. Make sure that children do not suck or eat the berries, mistaking them for sweets, as they are poisonous. The plant is a native of Brazil.

Plenty of humidity is important to prevent the berries from falling; a liberal

Plenty of humidity, and a good light will ensure that the Christmas cherry's glossy berries do not fall.

supply of water, a good light including sun, and temperatures of around 16°C (60°F) maximum, are other requirements.

Streptocarpus (Cape primrose)

If you want a trouble-free, flowering plant, then this is the one. The Cape primrose from South Africa starts to flower in early summer and is likely to be still flowering the following spring. If encouraged it would probably be an all-the-year-round plant, but it is a good idea to rest such enthusiastic plants at some stage during the growing cycle, otherwise they have a short life and flower themselves to death.

The flowers are carried singly or in clusters of three or four at the end of slender stems up to 30 cm (12 in) long; they are funnel shaped, 5 cm (2 in) wide, and coloured blue, violet, white, pink, magenta, and all shades of these colours.

There is also a lovely range which has darker feathering and pencilling in the throat, called the Concorde range, and another one, the Royal range, with larger flowers on shorter stems. The leaves can be more than 30 cm (12 in) long, from the base of the plant.

A cool temperature in summer is preferred, not more than 21°C (70°F), with a MWT of 7.5°C (45°F). Supply average humidity, a good light, but not sun (even a little shade), water well in summer, and liquid feed regularly.

The Cape primrose grows fast and may need repotting in mid summer. Propagation is easily managed by division at repotting time, in spring.

Thunbergia alata (black-eyed Susan)

A neat little climbing plant which does not get out of control, with unusual, flat, light orange flowers, black in the centre, and about 5 cm (2 in) wide.

Black-eyed Susan can grow to 2.4 m (8 ft) tall, but in practice can be kept at about 1.5 m (5 ft), by pinching out the tips of stems and restricting the root-ball in an 18-cm (7-in) pot. It can also be grown as a trailer. Varieties with yellow or white flowers are available. Flowering is from mid summer to early or mid autumn. The plant's home is tropical Africa.

Supply average summer temperatures, plenty of water and humidity, and a good light. Tie the plant to a trellis as it grows. The rhizome (underground creeping stem) can be kept over winter, if free of frost, and repotted in spring, but new plants from seed will give a better display.

Tropaeolum majus (nasturtium)

The nasturtiums are the ideal annual climbing plants for providing lots of colour in a short time, and for covering a lot of space. They do best with plenty of light, preferably sun, and grow well in glass porches, or rooms with plate-glass to floor level. There are also the small bushy varieties (T. m. nanum), of which the mixture called Alaska is a particularly good example, with leaves splashed and spotted with white.

Flower colours are all shades of orange, yellow, red, flame, salmon and mahogany, and flowering continues from mid summer until mid autumn. Nasturtiums are native to Peru.

Provide normal summer temperatures and humidity, and water well, but allow the compost to dry between waterings, and supply sunlight. Sow seeds in mid to late spring; put three climbing kinds of nasturtium in a 13-cm (5-in) pot, or two bushy ones in a 10-cm (4-in) pot.

Thunbergia alata's 'black eye' makes this a striking plant. It is adaptable to different habits of growth, such as climbing a trellis or trailing from a basket.

PLANTS FOR WINTER AND SPRING FLOWERING

Since many winter-flowering plants will be in the shops well before Christmas, you can have a really dramatic and colourful seasonal display. But often the display does not end there. Many plants will continue flowering into late winter; some of those which started in late winter will still be flowering in spring, and some of those which started flowering in late summer will carry on into winter. Amongst those plants which continue flowering into winter are: bouvardia, capsicum (ornamental pepper, fruit), fuchsia, pelargonium, saintpaulia (African violet), solanum (Christmas cherry, fruit), and streptocarpus (Cape primrose). Other winter- and spring-flowering plants include the orchids, pages 75–6, the rat-tail cactus, epiphyllum, page 70, and the Christmas and Easter cacti, page 74.

Anthurium
Exotic and bizarre-looking flowering plants, the anthuriums will be a talking point wherever they are grown. They originate in the tropical rain forests of South America, and need careful attention in order to reward you with their flamboyant flowers.

They have the typical flower of their plant family, consisting of one large 'petal' (spathe), from which a short vertical spike (spadix) extends. *A. scherzerianum* (flamingo flower) is the easier to grow of the two commonly available, and has a bright, shiny, red petal about 5 cm (2 in) in diameter, and a twisted spike; height is about 30 cm (12 in). *A. andreanum* is 60 or 90 cm (2 or 3 ft) tall; the petal is 10 cm (4 in) long and can be orange, pink, or white, depending on the variety. Flowering time for both is late winter, through spring.

Lots of humidity at all times is vital; MWT should be 16°C (60°F), while a good light but no sun is the summer requirement; a moist, but never waterlogged, compost should always be provided. Lukewarm, soft water is particularly important for these plants.

Aphelandra squarrosa (Zebra plant)
The zebra plant is one of the most architecturally interesting indoor plants, having stiff, erect stems about 38 cm (15 in) tall, from which white-veined, pointed leaves up to 13 cm (5 in) long grow in pairs. At the top of the stems there is a golden-yellow spike with tubular white flowers protruding from between each yellow bract. The flowers appear in early winter and die quite soon afterwards, but the bract lasts until well into mid winter. A smaller cultivar called 'Louisae' has red stems about 25 cm (10 in) tall. Aphelandras grow as evergreen shrubs in Brazil, their native country.

The zebra plants need lots of water while flowering, otherwise the leaves quickly wilt and fall, leaving a bare stem with a tuft of leaves at the top, as is so often seen on these plants. Humidity is vital, for the dry atmosphere of central heating soon turns the leaves brown at the edges.

Provide a good light, and a steady temperature of about 18–21°C (64–70°F), without draughts.

After flowering, when the leaves begin to change colour, cut the stems down to about 5 cm (2 in), give much less water and lower the temperature to about 13°C (55°F). After several weeks raise it, water normally, and repot when new sideshoots begin to grow. In summer and autumn use a liquid feed for good flowering.

Azalea
The modern varieties of azaleas grown as indoor pot plants have charmingly glamorous flowers covering a small, bushy, evergreen plant from late autumn to mid winter. In bloom, an azalea plant appears to be covered with masses of delicately coloured, crinkled tissue paper, in white, pink, pink and white, scarlet, salmon, crimson, and similar shades. These azaleas are hybrids bred from the Chinese

A draught-free, light environment and humidity are vital for the zebra plant to flourish. The strongly marked, prominent leaves stand out in any houseplant collection.

Of Chinese origin, azaleas form exotic winter showpieces.

A cool temperature is essential to ensure the camellia's profuse and gorgeous blooming in spring.

species, *Rhododendron simsii.*

Such an attractive plant deserves a lot of care, and it is quite possible to keep it indefinitely, flowering every winter. In flower, it needs watering every day with soft water if you have central heating and a dry atmosphere. Also provide lots of humidity with at least one daily misting, humidity trays or saucers, and other plants close by. A good light, and cool temperatures keep it flowering, round about 13°C (55°F) is ideal. Dry roots or dry air will result in leaf fall, and bud and flower drop.

After flowering, cut back the flowered shoots a little, to just above a side-shoot. By this time new shoots will already be starting to appear; cut the root ball down a little (not as much as for large plants, see page 84), repot with fresh acid compost in the same size or a slightly larger pot, with plenty of drainage material in the base, water in, and leave in a cooler but frost-free place. Maintain the watering, and in late spring put the plant outdoors in a shady place, with the pot buried up to the rim, for the summer. Give a fortnightly liquid-feed, and water during drought, then bring in before the autumn frost, stop feeding, and water moderately. The flower-buds should then soon appear.

Camellia

Camellias were once considered to be too tender to be grown anywhere but in a warm greenhouse or a conservatory, but they are hardy enough to grow outdoors in many sheltered gardens. They are ideal for containers, as they grow at a moderate rate, need no pruning, and have glossy evergreen, laurel-like leaves adorned with beautiful single or double flowers in pinks, reds, and white, also being striped and 'splashed' with these colours. Hybrids of *C. japonica,* from Japan, are the ones most commonly grown; *C. sinensis* is the plant whose leaves are used for making tea. Flowering is early, during March–April.

Keep the plant cool but frost-free in winter, and at about 13–16°C (55–60°F) while the buds are opening and it is in full flower. Temperatures in summer and autumn should be normal, but preferably not above 24°C (75°F). A good light, moderate watering with soft water, and average humidity are ideal. Repot when the container is full of roots, about every

Above: Leaves vanish beneath the cineraria's vivid, eye-catching flowers. Watch out for the voracious leafminer, to which a cineraria is caviar.

Right: Keep crocus bulbs in the dark from autumn, until shoot tips are 2.5 cm (I in) high.

two to three years, and use acid compost. Supply one dry feed of a potash-high fertilizer in mid summer and water in well. The flower buds start to appear in early autumn, but do not open until early spring.

Cineraria

There are not many flowering plants for indoors which belong to the daisy family. Most of this family is hardy, but the cineraria hybrids need protection, even though they are very nearly hardy. These gloriously coloured daisies are available in pinks, reds, blues, wine-red, and so on – the royal blue is an astonishing colour – and they cover the plants so completely that the leaves are hidden. Available in early winter, they light up dull winter days more than most other indoor plants.

The original species from which the hybrids have been developed comes from the Canary Islands.

Cool temperatures are most important, about 10°C (50°F), with a good light or a little shade, otherwise they finish flowering quickly, and get dreadfully infested with greenfly. Plenty of water and humidity are also necessary.

Look for greenfly round the buds and on the tips of shoots; also watch out for leafminer which appear, apparently from nowhere, and regard cinerarias as caviar! After flowering, the plants must be discarded, as they are annuals.

Citrofortunella mitis (calamondin)

Orange trees used to be grown indoors in the lovely forerunners of conservatories called orangeries, where they remained from mid autumn to late spring; in summer they were put outside in the sun. This tiny relation also bears oranges, but only about 4 cm ($1\frac{1}{2}$ in) in diameter, on a shrubby evergreen plant slowly growing to 1.2 m (4 ft) in its home in the Philippines, though much less in a container. The oranges are edible, but bitter, making good marmalade provided there are enough to be worth using. White, heavily fragrant flowers appear in spring, and the oranges hang on the plant in colours from green to orange depending on their maturity, for most of the year.

Water moderately while growing and keep on the dry side in winter, with a MWT of 10°C (50°F). Feed and mist regularly in the growing season – misting will help the

Unusual, reflexed petals, and silvery-grey leaves distinguish the cyclamen. Too much warmth is inimical to the plant's well-being, so keep it cool.

flowers to set fruit – and provide lots of light, including sun. Watch closely for scale insect and red spider mite.

Clivia miniata (Kaffir lily)
The Kaffir lilies are attractive spring-flowering plants with deep orange, lily-like flowers in clusters; each flower is about 7.5 cm (3 in) long, and there can be 20 in a cluster, on a stem 25 cm (10 in) tall. One plant can produce several offsets, each of which flowers, so it makes a tremendous display after a few years. Average humidity is satisfactory.

A good light but no sun and not too much water, moderate amounts while growing and much less in winter, will give good growth, together with cool winter temperatures, 4.5–7.5°C (40–45°F), which are essential to ensure flowering.

In the Kaffir lily's native South Africa the plant would be dry during our winter,

and flower in what is the autumn season there. Repot only when the container is crammed with roots, and then divide carefully as the roots are fleshy.

Crocus
There are crocuses which flower naturally outdoors in spring, and there are also crocuses – C. chrysanthus being the prettiest – which do so in late winter. The spring-flowering ones can be forced gently to bloom indoors in late winter, and in fact C. chrysanthus hybrids will flower early in mid winter. Colours are yellows, blues, purples and white, and you can buy named hybrids in autumn, or alternatively obtain bowls already planted up in early winter – they make a good Christmas gift. They come from eastern Europe.

When growing and flowering, keep the plants cool at about 10–16°C (50–60°F), water moderately, give a good light with

some sun, and average humidity. After flowering, continue to water, and start to liquid-feed the crocuses until the leaves die down, then leave dry and plant outdoors in the autumn.

If you are potting up your own bulbs, plant in peat-based compost in mid autumn, with the tip of each bulb just showing, and with 13 mm ($\frac{1}{2}$ in) between each one. Do not compress the compost beneath the bulbs. Water gently and put the container in total darkness (cover with black plastic sheet) in a cupboard with a temperature of 4.5–7.5°C (40–45°F). Keep the compost moist.

When the shoot tips are 2.5 cm (1 in) above the compost, bring the bowl into dim light and raise the temperature to 10°C (50°F) for a week or so. Thereafter, increase the light and temperature gradually as the flowerbuds develop.

Cyclamen
There are many species of cyclamen found growing wild in the eastern Mediterranean region, and C. persicum is the one from which the modern container plants have been bred. It has pointed petals and is strongly fragrant, but sadly the scent has been lost in the breeding, though the flowers are much larger and variously coloured pink, scarlet, magenta, white, salmon, crimson and purple.

Cyclamens are amongst the prettiest of the winter-flowering plants, and have very attractive leaves, marked in silvery white. A new miniature strain has been developed, which is often scented.

When in flower, water and mist daily if you have a dry atmosphere caused by central heating, but avoid splashing the tuber and top growth, especially the base of the stems.

Keep the plant in a good light, but not sun; the temperature should be cool, no more than 16°C (60°F). Liquid-feed at half-strength regularly while the plant is in leaf. Gradually dry off as the leaves turn yellow and wither, in late winter–early spring, then keep the cyclamen dry and warm in the pot until mid summer. Repot as soon as fresh leaves appear, half burying the tuber in new compost, and water. Then keep cool and well lit.

Yellowing leaves while growing mean either too much or too little water, too much light or too high a temperature.

Poinsettias provide scarlet splashes of colour to ornament the Christmas scene.

Erica gracilis (Cape heath)

There are many varieties and hybrids of our common heaths and heathers which grow on the moors and mountains throughout Britain, and flower in autumn and winter. But the majority of these plants come from South Africa, where they grow in a much warmer climate. Nevertheless, they still require to be kept relatively cool while flowering.

The Cape heath blooms from mid autumn to mid winter, when it covers itself in tiny, rose-pink, bell-like flowers. Out of flower it is a small, bushy plant with tough woody stems and tiny, light green, needle-like leaves which drop in showers in a hot, dry atmosphere; its height is about 45 cm (18 in).

The plant should always be kept cool while flowering, between 7.5 and 13°C (45 and 55°F), which is much lower than you will find comfortable, so a glass porch facing north or a barely-heated conservatory are probably the best places to put it in. A good light and acid compost are necessary, together with soft water and considerable humidity. In summer the Cape heath can be put outdoors in a warm, sunny place.

Euphorbia pulcherrima (poinsettia)

Poinsettias are shrubby plants from Mexico where they can grow 3 m (10 ft) tall, and flower in the autumn. By controlling the amount of light they receive in the autumn, they have been induced to produce their red flowers from early to mid winter; the most modern strains have pink or white flowers.

Although brilliantly attractive, poinsettias are not easily grown. The temperature surrounding them must be kept constant, without draughts, the MWT being 16°C (60°F), preferably higher. Provide a good humid atmosphere, and regular waterings with tepid water, but leave the compost to dry a little between each drink to the point where the leaves almost wilt. Plenty of light is also required.

To grow on, cut down after flowering to about 7.5 cm (3 in), keep dryish and warm till late spring, then repot in fresh compost. Provide water, a good light and begin to give a regular liquid-feed. From early autumn till early winter keep in the dark for 14 hours every night, to ensure flowers in early winter.

The cluster of enormous flowers gives amaryllis a dramatic presence. Look out for the 'Apple Blossom' hybrid, as well as this vermilion dazzler.

Hippeastrum (amaryllis)

The amaryllis, as it is popularly called, is one of the most beautiful of the flowering bulbs. Its enormous, trumpet-shaped flowers are 15 cm (6 in) wide, with either one or a cluster appearing at the top of a 30 cm (1 ft) stem. The colours vary from scarlet and orange to white, with one particularly lovely hybrid called 'Apple Blossom' being white and delicate pink. The strap-shaped leaves come from a bulb 10 cm (4 in) wide. From South America.

You can obtain prepared bulbs which will flower early in mid winter, having been planted at the start of winter, or normally treated ones which flower in spring, having been planted from mid to late winter. Bury only half the bulb in the compost, using a 15 cm (6 in) pot, water in well, and keep at about 21°C (70°F) with minimum watering until growth is obvious. Then supply moderate watering and a good light, average humidity and a slightly lower temperature. After flowering, take off the faded flowers, liquid-feed until the leaves die down, and keep dry, with a temperature of no lower than 4.5°C (40°F) until repotting time.

Hyacinthus (hyacinth)

Hyacinths must be amongst the most popular bulbs for indoor growing, especially those prepared for Christmas flowering. Their fat, heavily scented spikes of flowers last for several weeks, and are coloured in muted shades of blue, pink, red, yellow, orange, salmon and white – all the colours of the rainbow. By choosing carefully it is possible to have them in flower in succession from Christmas to well into early spring. These beautiful hybrids have been bred from a Mediterranean region species.

Plant the Christmas flowering varieties in early autumn, others from mid to late autumn. Put one in a 10 cm (4 in) wide container, or allow 2.5 cm (1 in) between bulbs planted in groups, and bury to leave the tip ('nose') protruding. Do not press down firmly, otherwise the roots will rise to the compost surface. Water in, place in a dark cupboard and keep at a temperature of 4.5°C (40°F). Bring out when the growth has put on 2.5 cm (1 in), provide a little warmth and shaded light, and gradually increase both, with the temperature reaching a maximum of 13°C (55°F).

Fragrance and intense, contrasting colours highlight *Iris reticulata*.

Iris reticulata

These delightful miniature irises from the Caucasus mountains of Russia are easily grown indoors in cool temperatures. Purple, blue, and shades of these colours, with bright orange 'beards' are typical; 'Harmony' and 'Cambridge Blue' are two of the named hybrids. Height is about 15 cm (6 in). They have the bonus of a sweet fragrance, and flower from mid or late winter, depending on the time of planting.

Plant the small round bulbs at the end of late summer for mid winter flowering, and in early autumn for later flowering. Space them 4 cm (1½ in) deep and 2.5 cm (1 in) apart, using a pan (half-pot) with drainage material in the base. Keep cool, 7.5°C (45°F), and shaded, but give as much light as possible when the leaves show, with a little more warmth. Keep dry in summer.

Jasminum polyanthum (jasmine)
If you are fond of jasmine's exotic fragrance, you can enjoy it in winter as well as summer by growing this Chinese species. Its white flowers open from pink-tinted buds in late autumn or early winter, and continue in succession until early spring. It is a vigorous climber, the height depending on the size of the container; one 20 cm (8 in) in diameter will result in a plant at least 1.8 m (6 ft) tall. The plant is a native of tropical Asia.

Provide normal temperatures in summer and a MWT of 4.5°C (40°F), but preferably in the range 18–21°C (65–70°F) while flowering. Plenty of water and light, including sun, is also required, and average humidity. Liquid-feed in summer with a potash-high fertilizer. Prune in spring, removing flowered shoots and cutting back the others if they have outgrown the space available. It flowers on shoots produced during the summer.

Pachystachys lutea (lollipop plant)
The lollipop plant, like the zebra plant, comes from Brazil, and therefore requires the same growing conditions. On the other hand it starts to flower in late spring and continues well into the autumn.

It too is a handsome plant, its 15-cm (6-in) long flower spikes resembling the sweets it is named after, being flat, conical and bright yellow. Its evergreen leaves are plain and not striped, on stems growing up to 45 cm (1½ ft) tall, of which there are perhaps seven or eight per plant.

As with the aphelandra, it needs a good light, but no sun, normal summer temperatures, and a MWT of 13°C (55°F). Provide plenty of water and good humidity while growing, but in winter keep it on the dry side. In late winter or early spring repot in fresh compost, cutting the stems down to approximately 3.5 cm (1½ in) in length, and either take tip cuttings from the new growth and root them, or grow the plant on to flowering stage.

Primula
The pot plant primulas are amongst the most attractive and easiest of plants to be grown in the home, and in winter there is nothing more evocative of the spring than

You can enjoy the scent of jasmine in winter as well as summer by growing *Jasminum polyanthum*. Make sure you have space for it. If planted in a 20-cm (8-in) container, it will climb 1.8 m (6ft).

their pretty, brightly coloured flowers.

The main differences between the species are the petal shapes; *P. obconica* has rounded, overlapping petals, *P. sinensis* has frilly edges to the petals, *P. malacoides* has delicate, almost starry flowers with a notch in the edge of each petal, and *P.× kewensis* is always bright yellow, fragrant, and with a marked tube behind the much smaller petals. Colours of the other three are in the range of pinks, blues, purple, orange and white. *P. obconica* sometimes causes a rash on the skin of people who are sensitive to it.

Keep primulas cool and well watered while flowering, in the 60sF, with some humidity and a good light, but no direct sun. Afterwards repot, divide if necessary, and keep in a little shade until the autumn, with little water, then provide a better light and more water.

Sparmannia africana (House lime)

An unusual plant for indoor gardening, in that it can be grown for the sake of both its foliage and flowers. The leaves are large, light green and soft to the touch, the flowers white and rounded, up to 3 cm (1½ in) wide, and centred with long golden, purple-tipped stamens, forming a brush. The whole plant can be 60 or 90 cm (2 or 3 ft) tall, and half as much wide; it flowers in early spring. Its native home is South Africa, where it will grow to 4.5 m (15 ft).

A good light all year with winter sunlight will encourage early flowering; average humidity and temperatures with a MWT of 7.5°C (45°F) suit it. Water should be plentiful in summer, very moderately applied in winter. Repot in spring and during the growing season, as it grows very fast; cut back after flowering to keep under control, and make it bushier, but if it still gets lanky, pinch out the tips of the new growth.

Spathiphyllum wallisii (peace lily, white sails)

The 'flower' of this plant lasts for several months and is a single, large, white, oval 'petal', properly called a spathe. The yellow spike which comes up from the base of the spathe is the spadix, and carries the pollen. The narrow, pointed, evergreen leaves grow on stems about 20 cm (8 in) long. The whole plant is only about 25 cm (10 in) high, but there is a larger version,

The long-flowering lollipop plant's curious blooms, give it personality. Good light is important for its growth, as is humidity.

The house lime's white flowers have long, golden, purple-tipped stamens, forming a brush.

'Mauna Loa', (the name of a resort in Hawaii) which will flower nearly all year round, given sufficient warmth. The plant comes from South America.

Spathiphyllums need lots of humidity all year round; sponging the leaves regularly helps, in addition to cleaning off dirt and dust. A MWT of 13°C (55°F) is needed, with normal summer temperatures. The light should be good in winter, and on the dull side in summer – never put it in a sunny place. Water well while growing, moderately otherwise. If you want more than one, the plant can be divided in spring, when repotting in fresh compost is also necessary.

PLANTS THAT FLOWER
ALL THE YEAR ROUND

Besides the plants which flower at particular seasons of the year, there are some which appear to be indifferent to temperature or light. If permitted, they flower all the year round. Others are considerably affected by the length of the daylight and, by carefully controlling this, together with the amount of warmth they receive, they can be made to flower out of season.

If you allow the all-the-year-round plants to flower continuously, they will have a shorter life than usual. They will need a good deal of liquid-feeding to keep them going, and more fresh compost. Even so there will be periods when the flowers are fewer, as might be expected.

Begonia
There are four main kinds of flowering begonias. First, the large double-flowered varieties in dazzling shades of red, orange, yellow, pink and white, and combinations of these, grown from tubers. Second, the small, single-flowered kind, mostly in pink, rose-pink or white, with green or wine-coloured leaves, which flower from early summer to late autumn, or all through winter, and which are fibrous-rooted. Third, double-flowered Rosebud types in similar shades, and the larger, double but open Rieger hybrids, which flower from autumn through winter into spring, and which are also fibrous rooted.

Fourth, the pendulous kinds with either single, quite large, pointed flowers, or single small flowers in large quantities, as in *B. sutherlandii*, coloured orange, and which grow from tubers.

All require good light or semi-shade, but never sunlight. Provide plenty of water while growing and flowering, but the tubers should be dried off in autumn, and kept dry, with a MWT of 7.5°C (45°F), until started into growth the following spring, with fresh compost and renewed watering, together with warmth. Those which flower through winter should still be watered and kept at about 18°C (65°F). The Rieger, Rosebud and small single-flowered kinds

are discarded once flowering has finished, though you can root tip-cuttings from them, if you would like further plants. All these types need good humidity.

The pendulous begonias are usually tuberous and should be treated as the large, double-flowered kind. In high temperatures they require frequent misting, otherwise normal humidity is enough. Begonias mostly come from South America.

Beloperone guttata (shrimp plant)
A small, bushy, evergreen plant with striking salmon-pink 'flowers' up to 7.5 cm (3 in) long, composed in fact of coloured bracts, from which come small white tubular flowers, spotted purple in the throat. The whole plant is soft to touch and slightly hairy. Its height will be about 30–45 cm (1–1½ ft), though in its native Mexico it can grow into a shrub 90 cm (3 ft) tall. You will sometimes come across a yellow form, called 'Yellow Queen'.

Give it a good light with some sun – which is important – water well from spring to autumn, moderately in winter, and supply average humidity and a MWT of 13°C (55°F). It will keep flowering if it is kept cooler at night than during the day. In order to rest the shrimp plant, you should lower the temperature a few degrees in winter and give much less water, until early spring. Then cut back by about half, repot in fresh compost and treat normally, when new shoots will appear. It roots easily from tip cuttings.

Chrysanthemum
Once grown only for its cut flowers or as border plants, there are now small bushy chrysanthemums which can be grown as pot plants, flowering continuously for many weeks. Such plants can be bought all the year round instead of only in summer, autumn and early winter, the normal flowering time. This is because their growth has been manipulated by the nurseryman with the help of day-length control; they are also treated with a chemical which keeps them small, at about 30 cm (1 ft) tall. The main colours are bronze, yellow, white – pink, purple and red are also available – and all their shades. The species from which they are derived originated in China and Japan.

Water well, provide good light and average humidity, together with cool temperatures of around 10–16°C (50–60°F), and plant them outdoors in late spring or summer when flowering is over. They will grow to a much taller height in the garden, and will also flower again.

Impatiens (busy Lizzie)
One of the most popular flowering indoor plants, the busy lizzies flower profusely without stopping, if given the chance. They have fleshy stems and flat, open flowers which come in shades of red, pink, orange, white, magenta and purple; recently a yellow flowering version has been introduced. The New Guinea hybrids have

Left: Begonias can be in flower in succession for all seasons. The double-flowered varieties are the most flamboyant.

Right: Pot chrysanthemums offer masses of long-lasting blooms.

41

highly ornamental leaves as well, variegated yellow and red on green. All are bushy plants between 20 and 45 cm (8 and 18 in) tall, sometimes more, and they come from tropical regions of the world, mainly the Far East and Africa.

Water well, especially in summer, and also over winter if you have central heating. Give a good light, with winter sun, and average humidity – but mist regularly in a centrally heated atmosphere. Supply a MWT of 16°C (60°F) for continued flowering. Prune in spring to cut the main stems back by half, repot in fresh compost, and pinch out the tips of new shoots to keep the plants bushy and floriferous. They root easily from tip cuttings, even in plain water. Watch for red spider mite.

Kalanchoe blossfeldiana

This species has produced hybrids with red (the most common colour), orange and yellow or creamy flowers; sometimes you will see lilac-coloured ones offered for sale. Kalanchoes will reach a height of between 20–38 cm (8–15 in). Whereas they were once only available at Christmas, now they can be bought all the year round. As with the chrysanthemum, the kalanchoe has been manipulated to flower even when it would not naturally do so.

Miniatures are also available with red or yellow flowers, such as 'Tom Thumb', growing to 10–15 cm (4–6 in) high, with a mass of tiny flowers. The leaves are fleshy and evergreen in their native Madagascar.

Myriad tiny blooms cluster on each of *Kalanchoe blossfeldiana's* flower-heads.

Easily grown, the MWT should not fall below 10°C (50°F), with average humidity, a good light with sun in winter, but not in summer, and moderate watering, so that the compost can become almost dry between waterings. You can encourage it to flower again by removing the dead flowerheads, resting it for a few weeks with lower temperatures, providing a little shade and hardly any water. Then start it off again with fresh compost and increased warmth, light and water.

PLAIN GREEN-LEAVED FOLIAGE PLANTS

The enormous advantage of foliage plants is that, being evergreen, they are decorative all year round. Also, green is a refreshing and peaceful colour; it is the colour associated with the outdoor garden and the countryside, and splashes of it in the home introduce a sense of tranquillity and freshness.

There are more shades of green than any other colour because it is in the middle of the spectrum. Therefore no two foliage plants will ever be the same green. But there is also a large group of foliage plants whose leaves are as vividly coloured as flowers – 'coloured', in this sense, meaning colours other than green. These are described in the next chapter.

Some of the plain green foliage plants have varieties with leaves variegated in white, cream or yellow; they are described for convenience's sake in this chapter, and listed at the end of the coloured-leaved plants in the next chapter. Some of the coloured-leaved varieties have plain green kinds such as: aglaonema, ivy, pteris and tradescantia.

Adiantum (Maidenhair fern)

The maidenhairs are graceful, arching ferns, happiest in a little shade and cool temperatures. The delicate and prettily shaped, light green leaves grow on black, wire-like stems in *A. capillus-veneris*, the most commonly grown species, which can reach 45 cm (18 in). It is found in cool temperate regions of the world.

A. raddianum 'Fragrantissimum', from Brazil, looks like a much smaller version, but has slightly scented fronds. *A. venustum* is quite different. It is a Himalayan fern with more conventional fronds, narrowly triangular and much more like the average fern, but coloured bronze-pink until they mature.

The most important point in the care of maidenhairs is the humidity of the atmosphere. The plants need lots of humidity, supplied either by misting several times a day, or by keeping them in a bathroom or kitchen, otherwise the thin filmy leaves turn brown, wither and die, in a matter of hours. Temperatures should be in the range 4.5–21°C (40–70°F), except for *A.* 'Fragrantissimum', which needs a MWT of 13°C (55°F). Moderate watering with soft water, and acid compost are required; repot each spring and also, when young, during the growing season.

Araucaria heterophylla (syn. *A. excelsa*) (Norfolk island pine)

The Norfolk island pine is a relative of the monkey puzzle tree, and comes from the tiny Pacific island of its common name, belonging to Australia, and 1280 km (800 miles) distant from New South Wales.

In the wild, it is a 60-m (200-ft) tree, but in containers remains a controllable size, eventually reaching about 1.8 m (6 ft), forming a neat evergreen with horizontal branches regularly arranged round the trunk in tiers. Its needle leaves form frond-like shoots, so that it looks more like a vertical fern with a central trunk.

Cultivation is easy, and the Norfolk island pine will thrive in a good light or a little shade, cool temperatures in winter (MWT 4.5°C, 40°F) with average warmth in summer, and normal humidity at all times. Water sparingly in winter, moderately in summer. Leaf fall indicates that the air is not sufficiently moist.

Asparagus

The asparagus fern is related to the vegetable asparagus, which itself has decorative fern-like foliage when allowed to grow to its full length. *A. densiflorus* 'Sprengeri' has long, trailing stems, decorated with needle-like leaves, from Natal, South Africa; *A. setaceus* (syn. *A.*

The asparagus fern is a decorative plant, extending feathery sprays of foliage, made up of thread-like leaflets.

plumosus), also South African, has flat, triangular 'leaves' consisting of stiff, thread-like leaflets, on equally stiff, wiry stems, which are much used by florists in formal bouquets.

You may come across a third variety, *A. meyeri*, the foxtail fern, with upright fronds about 45 cm (18 in) long in the best forms, made up of densely packed needle leaves – each frond looks more like a brush than anything else.

The asparagus ferns are not choosy plants, needing moderate watering, average humidity and a good light to some shade. Temperatures can be normal for the time of the year, with a MWT of 10°C (50°F), provided the night temperature is lower than that of the day time. Repot annually in spring, and cut straggling stems back to be replaced by new shoots.

Aspidistra elatior (cast-iron plant)

The merits of the aspidistra have been rediscovered in the last decade or so. It will grow in almost any environment except a really hot one, it stands any amount of neglect or wrong treatment except for heavy watering, and it is consistently handsome. Japan is its native home.

The plain green leaves are leathery and glossy, and can grow to 45 cm (18 in) long, pointed at one end and narrowing to the leaf stem at the other. There is a variegated variety, *A. e. variegata* with yellow-edged leaves, less easy to grow. Sometimes small purple growths appear at soil-level in early spring – these are its flowers, said to be pollinated by slugs.

Sponge the leaves occasionally to clean them of dust and dirt, supply average temperatures – MWT 4.5°C (40°F) – humidity and water, together with any degree of light from good to shady. Repot only occasionally in spring, every four years or so.

Asplenium nidus (bird's-nest fern)

The bird's-nest fern is one of the most handsome and unusual of the fern family. The leaf-like, undivided fronds of this plant grow to 20 cm (8 in) wide, and more than 90 cm (3 ft) long in its native tropical rainforests of Asia and South America, but in the home are more likely to be 30–45 cm (12–18 in) long.

The leafy fronds form an upright rosette down which rain runs to water the rhizomes; it grows like the bromeliads do (see the description given in the chapter on Special-care Plants, on page 66), as an epiphyte in the forks of trees, and can be hung in a macramé hanger, or bound on to bark and peat, also suspended.

Plenty of humidity, a MWT of 16°C (60°F), some shade and a peat-based compost suit the bird's-nest-fern best, together with overhead spraying so that the water runs down the centre of the leaves. Water moderately in summer, sparingly in winter. Repot in spring. Watch for scale insect and mealy bug.

This boldly variegated variety is not as easy to grow as the plain green-leaved aspidistra, which is an equally striking plant.

The fresh green of the asplenium fern conjures up its native tropical rain-forest. Humidity and overhead spraying go some way to reproducing its natural growing conditions.

Chamaedorea elegans (parlour palm)
The parlour palm is one of the easiest palms to grow, and increases steadily in size, growing all through the year, though more slowly in winter. It is one of the feather palms, with the leaves divided into narrow leaflets in pairs on opposite sides of the midrib. Its final size in a container is about 60 cm (2 ft), and within two or three years of obtaining it, depending on its original size, it will produce sprays of tiny round yellow flowers in early spring. It is native to Mexico.

The parlour palm will grow in good light to shade, normal temperatures, with a MWT of 10°C (50°F), preferably higher, and some humidity. Watering should be moderate in summer, and slightly less in winter. Repot every third year or so, when the container is full of roots, and top-dress in the spring of the other years. Watch for scale insect and red spider mite, and do make sure, when buying a palm, that it is not already infested.

Chrysalidopsis lutescens (areca palm)
The areca palm has the feather-like leaves of the parlour palm, but with a distinct yellow tinge. It is a more erect and alto-gether taller palm, growing to at least 1.5 m (5 ft), and with correspondingly larger leaves, as much as 90 cm (3 ft) long. Its close relative, *Areca catechu*, the betel palm, supplies the seed chewed by some Asians which turns the saliva red, and is thought to aid digestion. The areca palm is found in Mauritius. Cultivation of the areca palm is the same as that for the parlour palm.

Cissus
One of the more attractive and easily grown climbers is the Australian kanga-roo vine (*Cissus antarctica*). It grows about 30 cm (12 in) a year, sometimes more, and will eventually reach ceiling height. Its glossy leaves are toothed and dark green, rather like a large beech leaf, and it climbs by tendrils which coil around the nearest support, which indoors is usually a trellis.

Another species, the grape ivy *Cissus rhombifolia*, from Natal in South Africa, is frequently sold under the name of *Rhoicissus rhomboidea*, which is even more attractive. The leaves, 10 cm (4 in) long, are formed from three diamond-shaped toothed leaflets, which are glossy

and dark green. The plant climbs with the help of tendrils.

Its cultivar 'Ellen Danica' is a graceful variant, with deeply cut, toothed leaves. It is just as easily grown and, to my mind, more decorative. Both grow rapidly, ap-proximately by 1 m (3 ft) a year, but can be

'Ellen Danica' is a graceful variant of *Cissus rhombifolia*, with glossy, deeply cut leaves.

made thicker and more bushy if the shoots are constantly nipped back.

All these cissus should be grown with a little shade – light turns the leaves a sickly shade of yellowish green – and they do best in cool temperatures around the 16–18°C (60–65°F) mark, with a MWT of 4.5°C

The grape ivy, *Cissus rhombifolia* climbs exuberantly with the help of tendrils. *Cissus* like a little shade and cool temperatures.

45

Cissus antarctica, the Australian kangaroo vine, makes a stately ascent to the ceiling, at the rate of 30 cm (12 in) a year, sometimes more.

(40°F) for the grape ivy and 7.5°C (45°F) for the kangaroo vine. Average humidity and watering are all that is necessary, though repotting during the growing season may be required for the grape ivy (otherwise do it in early spring).

Cyanotis

You may not often come across these plants, which belong to the same family as the tradescantias and, like them, trail, though rather stiffly. *C. somaliensis*, pussy-ears, (from Somaliland) has deep green, pointed leaves sheathing the stems at their base, with long white hairs on the edges and tiny blue flowers like powder-puffs at the end of the stems in spring. The stems and leaves are fleshy.

Cyanotis kewensis, the teddy-bear vine (from India), is similarly succulent, but the whole plant is covered in thick reddish brown hair. Its purple flowers have a reddish tinge, and appear in late winter.

Both plants are easily grown and look good as hanging plants. Some sun will encourage flowering, and normal summer temperatures are suitable with a MWT of 10°C (50°F). Average humidity but not too much water are preferred. Water only sparingly in winter – the succulent nature of the plants means that they can store water, and too much in the compost will result in rotting. Divide when repotting in the spring.

Cyperus

The cyperuses are a kind of tropical sedge, with the two grown in containers being given the common name of umbrella plant or umbrella grass. The narrow leaves radiate from the top of the stems, like the spokes of an umbrella, and curve down-wards, the main difference being that those of *C. diffusus* are wider than those of *C. alternifolius*. However, the latter is twice the height, reaching about 2 m (6 ft).

A third species, not grown in the home because its height can be 3 m (10 ft) in the wild, is *C. papyrus*, from which the ancient Egyptians made parchment. They used the pith in criss-crossed overlapping strips, which were then pressed tightly together.

Above all, these plants are water-loving, and should be kept in saucers permanently filled with water so that the compost is always wet. They need normal summer temperatures, with a MWT of 10°C (50°F), good light to shade, and plenty of humidity. *C. diffusus* is tropical in origin, and *C. alternifolus* is a native of Madagascar.

Cyrtomium falcatum 'Rochfordianum' (holly fern)

A surprising number of ferns suitable for indoor gardening look most unlike the conventional fern, and the holly fern is one which particularly confounds expectations of a fern's appearance. The leaflets are just like holly leaves in shape (though they are not prickly), and are tooth-edged, dark green and shiny. The length of the leaves is about 30 cm (12 in) when fully grown. The holly fern originates from south-east Asia.

Grow it in peat-based acid compost, repot each spring until adult, and then wait until the rhizomes and roots fill the pot, ensuring that the rhizomes are only partly buried. Temperatures in the range 4.5–21°C (40–70°F) are preferred, together with average summer watering – the compost should always be moist but not water-logged – though less in winter, average humidity, and a good light or a little shade. Watch for scale insect.

Dionaea muscipula (Venus flytrap)

There are several carnivorous plants suitable for indoor gardening, and the Venus flytrap is one of them. It is grown more for its great interest than appearance.

Cyperus roots need to be kept permanently wet.

Each oblong leaf-blade is hinged in the centre and has a margin of teeth, with sensitive hairs on the upper side. When an insect lands on the hairs, the trap is triggered and the leaf folds together, with the teeth interlocking, so that the insect cannot escape.

Venus flytraps are found in South Carolina in North America, where they grow on damp, sandy soil. In flower they grow to about 15 cm (6 in). Otherwise the plants consist of a rosette of leaves close to the soil, each leaf, including the stalk, growing up to 15 cm (6 in) long.

They grow best in a shallow pot about 10–13 cm (4–5 in) wide. If the container is smaller than this at purchase, repot immediately. Use a mixture of half coarse sand and half moss peat, and keep in sun or a good light, standing in a saucer permanently containing water (see illustration on page 81, in the chapter on Caring for Indoor Plants). Supply a MWT of 10°C (50°F) and normal summer temperatures.

Dizygotheca elegantissima (false aralia)

An elegant vertical plant with several stems whose dark green, narrow leaflets have a bronzy tinge. They are deeply cut at the edges and radiate out from the top of a long leaf stalk. A well-grown plant is an eye-catching specimen, its distinctive leaves clothing the full length of the stems. It comes from the Pacific islands.

The false aralia needs careful cultivation. A steady temperature and a draught-free environment are essential, with normal summer warmth and a MWT of 16°C (60°F).

Plenty of humidity and a good light are also important, but the plant does not need a great deal of water while growing, and winter watering – when it is virtually dormant – should be sparing. Pot in spring but only in every second or third year.

A plant with teeth is naturally an object of great interest.

A form of *Fatsia japonica* with creamy white and pale green variegations in the centres of the leaves.

Fatsia japonica's dark green leaves are distinctively shaped.

Drosera capensis (sundew)

Like the Venus flytrap, this is a carnivorous plant, obtaining its mineral nutrients by digesting a variety of insects. The sundew (from South Africa) is usually grown in containers, but there are species native to Britain, which naturally grow, like it, in boggy places.

Insects are trapped by red sticky tentacles on the upper surface of the leaf, which gradually fold over so as to contain the insect more effectively. The green leaf-blade is about 4 cm (1½ in) long, and the leaves form a rosette at soil-level, with rosy pink flowers being produced on a stem about 30 cm (12 in) tall in summer.

The best growing medium is chopped living sphagnum moss. Use a 13 cm (5 in) pot, and keep it in a saucer permanently filled with water. Supply sunlight and a MWT of 10°C (50°F) with normal summer temperatures.

x **Fatshedera lizei** (ivy tree)

This is a hybrid between the Irish ivy, *Hedera helix* 'Hibernica', and *Fatsia japonica* 'Moseri', a nearly-hardy plant from Japan. The leaves are like giant ivy leaves, growing up to 25 cm (10 in) long. The plant can have the ivy's climbing habit, if grown up a moss-stick, and will reach about 1.8 m (6 ft). Alternatively, it can be made to grow like a bush by removing the tips of the shoots, which will keep it shorter but wider. Small round heads of green flowers appear in mid to late autumn. There is a variety called 'Variegata', the edges of whose leaves are creamy white.

Care of this handsome plant is easy, provided you remember that it is nearly hardy. It requires cool temperatures not above 21°C (70°F) in summer, humidity, a good light or a little shade, and not too much water to keep it thriving. However, hot dry atmospheres and sun will result in yellowish leaves, and attacks of red spider mite so keep an eye on its health.

Fatsia japonica (false castor oil plant)

The true castor oil plant is *Ricinus communis*, whose seeds are taken as a purgative. Although the fatsia does not produce these seeds, its leaves are much like those of the ricinus, palmately shaped with seven–nine lobes. Dark green and glossy, they can be as much as 40 cm (16 in) wide, making it a handsome and imposing plant. In a container the plant will grow to about 1.2–1.5 m (4–5 ft), but out of doors 1.8 m (6 ft) is not unusual in sheltered positions. In mid–late autumn it has large clusters of small white flowers in round heads. The variegated form ('Variegata') is unexpectedly striking, having white tipped leaf lobes.

Fatsia grows quickly and will probably need repotting during the growing season. Keep it well watered and in a good light, or a little shade, and supply average humidity and a MWT of 4.5°C (40°F) – a little

lower occasionally will do no harm. Pinch back the tips of shoots to make it bushier, and watch for scale insect.

Ficus

The post-war interest in indoor plants probably took off with the widespread introduction of the rubber plant *F. elastica*, a tree originally grown commercially for the rubber-supplying sap obtained from the trunk.

The large, oval, glossy leaves clothing vertical stems are long familiar, but now

there are variations on the original species. They include 'Black Prince', whose leaves are so deep red as to be almost black; 'Doescheri', with leaves patched in grey-green and dark green, edged with white, and pink-tinted midribs when young; and 'Schrijvereana', largely yellow-variegated with dark green patches.

There are other ficus species for indoor gardening – *F. elastica* is by no means the only one – and the Indian *F. benjamina* is one of the more delightful. It grows quickly into a graceful, tree-like plant, the height being restricted only by the size of the container and the height of the room. It has glossy pointed leaves, averaging 5–7.5 cm (2–3 in) long, in weeping sprays.

F. lyrata, the fiddle-leaf fig, comes from West Africa, and is notable for its large, fiddle-shaped leaves up to 60 cm (2 ft) long. *F. diversifolia*, the mistletoe fig, is Indian in origin, and has leaves unusually shaped for the genus, being almost circular. It also has round, yellow, fruit-like 'flowers', inside which are the minute true flowers – the outside eventually becomes the fruit, and in this respect is like the familiar edible fig, *F. carica*. The creeping fig, *F. pumila*, and the trailing fig, *F. radicans*, with larger, pointed leaves, make good trailing plants, the latter particularly in its variegated ('Variegata') form with creamy yellow edges.

In general the ornamental figs need a MWT of 10°C (50°F) – though higher for the small-leaved types – a good light, especially if variegated, but a little shade for the trailing kinds. Give a moderate to sparing watering, depending on the season, and average humidity, except for the trailing kinds and *F. benjamina*, which need frequent misting. Do not repot too often, every two or three years is sufficient. Watch for scale insect, especially on *F. benjamina*, and red spider mite on the small-leaved varieties.

Grevillea robusta (Australian silk-bark oak)

In their native countries many house-plants are large shrubs or giant forest trees. It is rarely appreciated that their natural height may be 30 m (100 ft) or more. The silk-bark oak, though it is a delightfully ornamental plant reaching about 3 m (10 ft) tall in containers, is 50 m (170 ft) tall in its native New South Wales,

A permanent sheen on the rubber plant's large, oval leaves contributes to its appeal.

in Australia. The graceful ferny leaves are 15–45 cm (6–18 in) long, and are its main ornament when grown as a pot plant; the adult trees produce yellow flowers.

The plant requires a good light, with sun in winter, average humidity, watering, and summer temperatures, with a MWT of 4.5°C (40°F). The occasional drenching in a warm summer shower will keep it clean and refreshed. Watch for red spider mite.

Heptapleurum arboricola

This is a relatively new plant for the indoor garden, grown widely only during the last 10–15 years. Its upright habit consists of one or several stems whose bark is bright green, clothed with umbrella-like leaves. Each narrow, shiny, bright green leaflet radiates from a single point on the leaf-stalk, and growth is rapid, at least 60 cm (2 ft) a year. There is one variety which has

leaves splashed and patched with an abundance of cream; it is called 'Variegata'.

Heptapleurum arboricola is not a demanding plant – average humidity, plenty of water in the growing season, a good light or a little shade, and a MWT of 10°C (50°F) are all it really needs. A soaking in a summer shower will keep the leaves clean. Pinch back the tip of the main shoot to produce a bushy plant rather than a tree 2.4 m (8 ft) tall. Watch for scale insect.

Howea forsteriana (syn. *Kentia forsteriana, Kentia palm*)

The Kentia palm is easily grown; like the parlour palm (*Chamaedorea elegans*), it has feathery leaves, but is likely to grow much taller. Each leaflet is broader, 2–2.5 cm (¾–1 in) wide, and the stems carrying the leaflets are more upright. It

grows more quickly, too and, unlike the parlour palm, will probably not flower. If you have the space, as in a conservatory, it will grow into an outstanding specimen plant, but even in a more confined position, is still a very attractive pot plant.

The Kentia palm is ideal where there is not much light, as it naturally grows in the shade of other trees when young, in its native home of Lord Howe island in the Pacific. Plenty of warmth in summer, and a MWT of 10°C (50°F) are required, but keep it below 16°C (60°F) at night in winter, otherwise red spider mite, scale insect and leaf drop will occur, as they are equally likely to do in dry atmospheres. Water moderately in summer, sparingly in winter; do not repot unless the container is almost cracking with the quantity of roots, and then do so in spring. Disturb the root ball as little as possible.

Heptapleurum arboricola 'Variegata' has leaves liberally splashed with cream.

Vast, slashed leaves and great height give the Swiss cheese plant an assured prominence in the indoor garden.

Monstera deliciosa (Swiss cheese plant)
The Swiss cheese plant is one of the most striking and dramatic indoor plants, which, combined with its height, ensures that it will never be short of attention. The large leaves can be more than 60 cm (2 ft) wide, and are deeply slashed from the margins, allegedly because the hurricane force winds of the tropics can blow through them without damage.

The Swiss cheese plant climbs to at least 1.8 m (6 ft), and needs a moss-stick to provide a home for its long aerial roots. A smaller version is sold as 'Borsigiana', correctly *M. pertusa*.

Keep the leaves well sponged and free of dust and grime, and provide a MWT of 10°C (50°F), preferably higher, with plenty of humidity if you have central heating. Subdued light or a little shade are adequate for its successful growth, together with sparing watering in winter, and moderate amounts in summer, when you should allow the plant to become almost dry between waterings. Remove the growing tip to control the height.

Nephrolepis

The nephrolepis are a lovely collection of easily-grown tropical ferns, meriting positions as specimen plants. *N. exaltata* 'Bostoniensis' is a particularly attractive plant, with bright green fronds 60 cm (2 ft) and more long, arching all round the container. It looks excellent growing in hanging baskets.

'Fluffy Ruffles', 'Whitmanii', and a number of other nephrolepis varieties, all have variations to the fronds and grow less rapidly. 'Bostoniensis' can grow from a small plant 15 cm (6 in) high in spring, to 45 cm (18 in) by the following spring.

Some shade, cool temperatures, average humidity and watering, and an acid, peat-based compost suit it well. Minimum winter temperature should be about 10°C (50°F). Give a fortnightly liquid-feed from mid summer until mid autumn.

Use the runners freely produced for increase, burying them well and growing on the resultant plantlets when well rooted. Also use the small, round balls on the roots, with a frond attached.

Pellaea rotundifolia (button fern)
Another atypical fern in appearance, the button fern does at least have fronds about 30 cm (1 ft) long when fully grown. However, each division of the frond is an entire, round, leathery segment, about 13 mm ($\frac{1}{2}$ in) wide, carried in pairs opposite one another along the midrib. Since the fronds arch over it is a low-growing fern, almost ground-covering. Its native country is New Zealand.

The button fern needs a little shade, and a MWT of 4.5°C (40°F), with cool summer temperatures. Water very moderately, sparingly in winter; humidity is not important, but a peat-based acid compost is, together with soft water.

Philodendron

The variation in leaf shape amongst the philodendrons is remarkable, and fully justifies their popularity as plants for container cultivation in the home. There are two leaf types: one which tends to be pointed, longish and almost spear-shaped, growing to 15 or 20 cm (6 or 8 in), and one which is 30 or 60 cm (1 or 2 ft) long and so much incised and indented at the edges as to be fern-like in some cases.

The best known philodendron is the sweetheart plant, *P. scandens* (a rampant climber from the forests of the West Indies and Central America) which supports itself by means of aerial roots, hence a moss-stick is advisable. The bright green, glossy leaves are heart-shaped, 30 cm (12 in) long when fully grown, but they are usually much smaller than this in containers.

It is an excellent plant for shade. There are several other species of climbers, even more decorative, but less easily grown, one of which is *P. melanochryson*. It comes from Colombia, and has velvety, olive green leaves with a golden sheen. Provide a MWT of 16°C (60°F).

The Brazilian *Philodendron bipinnatifidum* is non-climbing. Its height is about 1.2 m (4 ft) in a container, and it has large, dark green leaves about 45 cm (18 in) long when fully grown. They are deeply incised at the edges, so that it is almost as dramatic as the Swiss cheese plant.

Another popular non-climber is called *P. selloum*, with huge leaves growing to 90 cm (3 ft) long, so deeply indented that the midrib is almost reached, to produce narrow toothed segments.

Nephrolepis exaltata 'Bostoniensis' sprays out into bright green, arching fronds.

A remarkable variation in leaf shape is found in philodendrons.

Water sparingly in winter, and far more generously in summer, but do not swamp the plant. Provide plenty of humidity, especially in central heating, and a MWT of 10°C (50°F), unless otherwise noted, together with a good light or a little shade – *P. melanochryson* always needs a good light. Repot every second or third year.

Phoenix roebelinii (pigmy date palm)
It is possible to grow the date palm, *P. dactylifera*, from a date stone, but it is not as ornamental and soon becomes un-wieldy. The smaller version is much more satisfactory, with more delicate fronds arching over, and reaches a height of about 90 cm (3 ft) in a container. It comes from south-east Asia.

Growth is good if a little shade is provided, with a MWT of 10°C (50°F). Water moderately in summer, but give less in winter; ensure that compost drainage is good by putting a layer of crocks in the base of the container, whether this is made of clay or plastic. Average humidity with summer-rain showers will keep off red spider mite and scale insect.

Platycerium bifurcatum (stag's-horn fern)
It is extraordinary how many variations there are on fern fronds, and how much they can vary from the conventional frond shape. The stag's-horn fern is particularly arresting in appearance as it has entire, leathery fronds covered in a white down which fork, and then fork twice more so that they closely resemble the animal of their common name. These fertile fronds emerge from green, plate-like, overlapping sterile fronds, which wrap themselves round the support, or build up into a cone-like structure which becomes pale brown and papery.

The stag's-horn fern is an epiphyte (a plant that gains its nutrients and moisture from the air and rain), and will therefore grow best on a 'raft', or bound to a piece of cork-bark, both hanging in mid air. A native of tropical rain-forests it needs plenty of humidity, a little shade, an occasional thorough watering, and a MWT of 10°C (50°F). Feeding is not re-quired, and the stag's-horn fern does well in a mixture of peat-based compost and sphagnum moss. Watch for scale insect, to which it is very prone.

A graceful show is made by the pigmy date palm, *Phoenix roebelinii.*

53

Radermacheria

One of the most recent introductions to indoor gardening, these plants come from tropical south-east Asia, and are normally fast-growing, evergreen trees. Even in containers they are quick to grow, and 'Danielle' (the one most commonly seen) will grow about 30 cm (12 in) a year. The fern-like leaves consist of glossy, pointed leaflets each about 5 cm (2 in) wide and long, held out horizontally from the central stem, and forming a graceful and elegant small tree, quite distinct from the others grown indoors.

Unusually, it does not mind dry air, though it always benefits from misting. A good light, average watering, and a MWT of 13°C (55°F) suit it, with normal summer temperatures. Sponge the leaflets occasionally, and watch for scale insect.

Schefflera actinophylla

In Australia and Java this schefflera grows into an evergreen shrub up to 1.8 m (6 ft) tall, and as wide. In containers, 90 or 100 cm (3 or 3½ ft) is more likely, with less spread. The finger-like leaflets radiate out from a central point on the leaf-stem, and are about 23 cm (9 in) long and 7.5 cm (3 in) wide, coloured a bright shining green. Remove the growing tip to prevent it from getting lanky.

Though it needs a MWT of 13°C (55°F), it does not like high summer temperatures and does best in the range of 16–21°C (60–70°F). Water well in summer, but very moderately in winter, supply plenty of humidity, and a good light or a little shade. Pot in alternate springs.

Sedum sieboldii

This Japanese succulent plant is one of the more delightful foliage plants for hanging baskets or pots hanging from brackets on walls. The rounded, toothed, blue-green leaves are produced in threes along the 23 cm (9 in) stems.

In the autumn they gradually turn pinkish-purple, and at the same time clusters of tiny pink flowers open at the end of the stems. It dies down in early winter in cool temperatures, and will survive a little frost, sprouting again towards the end of late winter. The variegated form 'Medio-variegatum' has a pale yellow blotch in the centre of each leaf.

A good light with some sun is essential.

The appealingly-named piggy-back plant forms a mounded shape.

Humidity is not important, and watering should be normal in summer – allow the plant to almost dry out between waterings – but give very little in winter. Summer temperatures can be normal, with a MWT of 4.5° (40°F).

Tolmiea menziesii (hen-and-chickens plant, piggy-back plant)

This is a small evergreen plant with light green, heart-shaped leaves, toothed at the edges, which forms a mounded plant, but with one or two long stems hanging down. Plantlets form on the top of the leaves at the point where the leaf-stalk joins the leaf-blade, and the whole plant will be about 15 cm (6 in) tall and a little wider. It grows wild in north-west America.

As it is almost hardy, the MWT can be 4.5°C (40°F) or a little less, with cool summer temperatures and a maximum of 21°C (70°F), a good light or a little shade, and average humidity and watering. Cool, moist conditions will prevent red spider mite attacks.

Trachycarpus fortunei (windmill palm)

The windmill palm is one of the fan palms, from China, which can be grown outdoors in sheltered places in the south-west of Britain. It thrives much better indoors with a steady warmth, but needs plenty of space as the leaves can grow at least 60 cm (2 ft) in diameter, and are carried on stalks more than 45 cm (18 in) long.

Be careful with the drainage – add more grit if you are using John Innes potting compost – and put a layer of crocks at the base of the pot. Do not repot until the container is full of roots – in other words avoid disturbing the plant more than can possibly be helped. Water sparingly in winter, normally in summer, and keep it in a little shade or a good light, with normal summer temperatures and a MWT of 10°C (50°F). Keep well misted and humid, and watch for scale insect.

Yucca elephantipes

There are yuccas which are grown outdoors in warm gardens for the sake of their massive spikes of white bellflowers, but this one, grown indoors, is a foliage plant, sometimes called a false palm. The narrow leaves reach up to 1.2 m (4 ft) long when it grows wild in Central America, though they will be smaller in the home, forming a drooping cluster at the top of the thick, short trunk.

In a modern white or aluminium cylindrical container, the yucca is a dramatic specimen plant growing approximately 1 m (3 ft) tall, and meriting a place by itself. Flowers may be produced, if you are lucky, but it will take several years before they appear.

A large, deep, well-drained container is important, together with plenty of sun, a MWT of 7.5°C (45°F), and average humidity. Water well while growing, and keep on the dry side in winter. Repot in alternate years.

'COLOURED'-LEAVED PLANTS

There is really no excuse for not having as colourful a display of plants in the indoor garden as in the outdoor one, because there are so many foliage plants, as well as flowering ones, which have brilliantly coloured leaves. Some are in elementary colours, such as red or yellow; some are shades of green – blue-green, yellow-green, grey-green. Others are multicoloured, such as the flame nettles (*coleus*) or crotons (*codiaeum*). These, too, can be 'evergreen', and do not need to be replaced when the season ends, as with flowering indoor plants. The plants in the list that follows are all grown primarily for the colours of their leaves, though many also have the interesting shapes associated with the plain green-leaved varieties.

Don't forget that there are flowering indoor plants which have coloured leaves, and they include: aechmea (the urn plant), and the variegated ananas (pineapple); aphelandra; cryptanthus (starfish bromeliad); cyclamen; episcia; the variegated hibiscus; many of the impatiens, especially the New Guinea hybrids; and some of the pelargoniums. To this list you can further add variegated forms of the plain green kinds, such as the variegated aspidistra, fatshedera, fatsia, ficus, heptapleurum, and sedum.

Aglaonema (Chinese evergreen)

The type plant, *Aglaonema commutatum*, has handsome large leaves, with white, herringbone stripes, and its varieties are even more interesting. There are several of these, such as 'Pseudobracteatum' (yellow markings), 'Silver Queen', (nearly all silvery white), and 'Silver Spear', (creamy white markings). *A. pictum* is smaller, with deep green leaves marked in grey and blue-green. The size of its leaves is 20 × 5 cm (8 × 2 in), whereas those of the commutatum varieties is about 30 cm (12 in) long, and up to 7.5 cm (3 in) wide. The plants originate in south-east Asia.

Careful all year round cultivation is required. The plant needs a high MWT of 16°C (60°F), and plenty of humidity is also vital, involving frequent misting. Keep the plant in a little shade, and water sparingly in winter, giving good waterings in summer, between which it should become almost dry. Pot infrequently, about every third year, and use a wide container with a good drainage layer.

Begonia

Begonias make ideal plants for the indoor garden, whether they are grown for their flowers or foliage. Most of them come from Central and South America, some from south-east Asia, but wherever their origins they do not like direct sunlight, and some only grow really well in shade.

Amongst the foliage begonias some of the most interesting are a modern range of hybrids called the Caribbean Islands Mixed, with such names as 'Cleopatra' (deep brown-green, palm-shaped leaves), and 'Tiger' (brown-spotted, rounded leaves). Varied and striking, they have been specially bred for indoors, and grow quickly, though they never reach more than 15 × 30 cm (6 × 12 in).

These begonias are easier to care for than the Rex hybrids, nevertheless the latter are outstandingly attractive, with beautifully coloured leaves in shades of wine, pink, purple, green, brown and yellow. 'Silver Queen' is unusual in having silvery-green leaves, edged and centred with dark green. All the Rex hybrids have pointed, assymetrical leaves, on average reaching a size of 15 × 10 cm (6 × 4 in).

There are two other small bushy

A steady temperature, subdued light and moderate watering will prolong the life of *Begonia rex*, admired for its conspicuous markings.

begonias with ornamental leaves. The iron cross begonia, *B. masoniana*, has a dark brown marking on the leaf surface, which is unusually crinkled and corrugated. And *B. boweri*, an endearing little plant, is called the eye-lash begonia because of the hairs on the brown-spotted margins. The size is the same as that of the Caribbean hybrids, and it has white flowers in late winter.

Some of the large cane begonias are grown mainly for their foliage; expect them to grow to at least 1.5 m (5 ft), with a spread of 76 cm (2½ ft). *B. corallina* has white blotches on the upper side of the olive-green leaves, which are wine-red beneath, and produces red flowers in spring. *B. haageana*, the elephant's-ears begonia, has large leaves, hairy on both surfaces, with deep red undersides and hairy red stems. Its pink flowers open in winter making it one of the most handsome, superb specimen plants.

B. maculata is another shrubby begonia, but much less tall at 60–90 cm (2–3 ft). It has an abundance of white spots on the olive-green upper surface of its leaves, which are red beneath.

Humidity is important for begonias – they need plenty of it all the year round, otherwise their leaves rapidly brown and wither. Steady temperatures are also important, and they will even withstand relatively low ones in winter provided they are steady, and the compost is dryish. The MWT should be 13°C (55°F), but they will stand less than this for short periods. Provide all begonias with subdued light, and water moderately, though sparingly in winter. When they are more than four years old, cut up the rhizomes, and repot the youngest pieces in new compost.

Breynia nivosa (snow bush)

A new and very welcome addition to indoor gardening, although this Pacific Islands' plant was widely grown in greenhouses during the last century.

The snow bush has taken well to home growing, and in containers is a small, shrubby plant whose oval leaves are almost completely covered with white, hence its common name. There is a pretty variety, with the common name of leaf flower, in which the leaves are mottled red, pink, white and green.

A good light – but not sun, good

This group includes a calathea, a variety of devil's ivy and *Cordyline terminalis*.

humidity, a MWT of 13°C (55°F) – more if possible – in addition to normal watering in summer and sparing watering in winter, will keep the plant in good condition.

If the leaves curl and brown, increase the humidity and frequency of misting.

Calathea makoyana (peacock plant)

There are several varieties of calathea (which originates from Brazil) available, but this is the one most often stocked, and the easiest to grow, though it is not a beginner's plant.

However, the peacock plant is so attractive, with its long silvery green leaves, that it is worth trying to cultivate it. The length of the upright leaf blades is about 23 cm (9 in); they have dark green blotches on the upper side in a regular patterning, while they are deep red on the underside.

To maintain the leaf colour and prevent yellowing, keep the plant in a little shade and provide lots of humidity all year round. Steady temperatures are important – no night drops – with a MWT of 16°C (60°F). Water normally, but always use lukewarm water, never cold. Watch for red spider mite and leaf browning, which quickly cause trouble if the air is dry.

Ceropegia woodii (hearts-entangled)

South Africa is the home of many succulent plants, including this one, though it is not at all like the majority. It can be grown as a creeping plant, but is more attractive as a trailer when its 60–90 cm (2–3 ft) long stems hang down from a basket, wall or hanging pot. It grows from a tuber, and has deep purple stems clothed in pairs of thick, heart-shaped leaves about 13–20 mm (½–¾ in) wide, being silvery grey marked on dark green with reddish undersides. The summer flowers are tubular, deep purple with light purple tips, 13 mm (½ in) long, and are carried upright from the leaf joints.

Provide a good light – the better it is the more likely the plant is to flower – a MWT of 7.5°C (45°F), average humidity and sparing water in winter; in summer water well, then allow to almost dry out. Cut the stems back if they become straggly.

Chlorophytum comosum
'Variegatum' (spider plant)

This almost hardy familiar plant is South African in origin. Its long, narrow, pointed leaves are edged with wide bands of white, and arch over from a central point at ground level. Long stems are produced from the centre, which end in plantlets or white flowers, making it look particularly attractive hanging or as a pedestal plant. It produces a matted mass of fleshy, almost tuberous roots.

Keep in a good light, with average humidity, plenty of water in summer, less in winter, and a MWT of 4.5°C (40°F). Note that brown tips to the shoots are a sign of dry compost, and that greenfly invade it in poor light and erratic watering. Repot frequently, as it grows fast.

Codiaeum (croton)

If you want a spectacularly coloured foliage plant for indoor gardening, then crotons are amongst the best. Their glossy leaves are variously striped, spotted and blotched with yellow, pink, orange, red and green, and they are also segmented and incised into striking and dramatic shapes. In the tropics they are used as specimen shrubs or clipped into hedges. In containers a single plant usually grows to about 60 cm (2 ft) with several stems, making it nicely bushy.

Crotons need expert care, and if plagued by low temperatures or not enough water in the compost they will lose their lower leaves. Provide a MWT of 16°C (60°F) and keep well watered in the growing season, with lots of humidity at all times – which is very important – and water sparingly in winter. Always use lukewarm water. The light should always be good to maintain the leaf colour, and a little sun early or late in the day is helpful.

Coleus (flame-nettle)

These annual plants from Java provide a show from late spring until mid autumn, and are so vividly coloured as to outshine flowering plants. You can grow them from seed if you can supply a germinating temperature of 18°C (65°F), and you will get a much greater selection of colours and leaf shapes than by buying them as established plants.

The original type has nettle-shaped leaves, but the hybrids can be oak-leaved shaped, frilly, ruffled, and long-pointed or wavy-edged. Colours include pink, magenta, brown, red, yellow, white, and green, and the leaves are usually multi-coloured, though sometimes only bi-coloured. Blue flower spikes appear if the shoot tips are not removed.

The spider plant's arching stems end in appealing plantlets.

A good light is vital to maintain the croton's spectacular leaf colour.

Dieffenbachia picta 'Exotica' is spectacularly splashed with white. The dumb canes need plenty of humidity and frequent misting.

Keep in a very good light, but avoid midday summer sun. Water freely, and supply average humidity and summer temperatures. The lack of light in winter means that the colours fade, so they are not worth keeping.

Cordyline

These are upright growing plants, sometimes called false palms, from tropical Asia. *C. terminalis* and its varieties are those most often seen. The handsome leaves are arranged in rosettes on gradually elongating stems, and can be more than 30 cm (12 in) long, and about 10 cm (4 in) wide, splashed and marked with yellow, pink, red, bronze and purple on dark green. The varieties include 'Tricolor' (cream, pink and red); 'Firebrand' (bronze); and 'Rededge' (red margins).

The Ti or Happy plants can be cordylines, grown from a piece of dried stem. Plenty of humidity and water are necessary while growing; in winter reduce the amount of water but still keep the compost moist, while maintaining some humidity.

Dracaenas prefer a little shade; good humidity and moist compost are other requirements.

A little shade suits them, but with occasional sun, a normal summer temperature and a MWT of 13°C (55°F) occasionally dropping to 10°C (50°F).

Cordyline australis, from New Zealand, produces a rosette of narrow, arching leaves eventually growing up to 1.2 m (4 ft) tall, and about 75 cm (2½ ft) wide on top of a slowly elongating stem. It will grow in average humidity, and a MWT of 10°C (50°F); otherwise, treat as for *C. terminalis*.

Dieffenbachia (dumb cane)

The dumb canes are large plants, and when grown well have broad leaves up to 25 cm (10 in) long and 10 cm (4 in) wide. Varieties of *D. picta* are the ones usually seen, such as 'Tropic Snow' (creamy white striping in the centre), 'Marianne' (nearly all white), and 'Exotica', (heavily splashed with white).

In good conditions a plant can grow to 1.8 m (6 ft), its leaves clothing most of the trunk, making it a most effective specimen. The plant comes from South America, and gets its common name from the fact that if chewed its poisonous leaves cause considerable pain to the mouth and lips.

Plenty of humidity, with frequent misting, is essential all the year round. In summer provide normal temperatures, a good deal of water, and a little shade. Winter conditions should include a MWT of 16°C (60°F) and much more light, since winter sunlight in Britain is generally weak, and sparing amounts of water. Draughts, dry compost and cold result in discoloured leaves and brown leaf edges.

Dracaena

The variation in leaves between members of this plant group is considerable, both in shape and habit, as well as colour. Most of those grown in the home come from the African continent. *D. surculosa* (syn *D. godseffiana*) is a shrubby plant with rounded, heavily white-spotted leaves, of which 'Florida Beauty' is a particularly good version. *D. fragrans* 'Massangeana' is yellow-striped down the middle of glossy, arching leaves 45 cm (18 in) long in a rosette. *D. marginata* 'Tricolor' is very narrow-leaved, edged with yellow and pink, forming a rosette on top of a thin trunk several feet tall. And *D. sanderana* has grey-green, pointed leaves about 5 cm (2 in) wide, edged with cream.

Shiny, heart-shaped leaves and pale yellow variegation characterize the devil's ivy.

A little shade is preferred, normal summer temperatures, a MWT of 13°C (55°F), and good humidity except for *D. surculosa*, which will withstand a dry atmosphere. Water well while growing, sparingly in winter, but keep moist – dry compost results in leaf drop.

Epipremnum aureum (devil's ivy)

A handsome fleshy climber from the Solomon islands, whose heart-shaped leaves are thick, glossy, and irregularly variegated pale yellow. The leaves achieve a length of about 12 cm (5 in), and are nearly as wide.

'Golden Queen' is a variety whose leaves are nearly all yellow; 'Marble Queen' is white variegated – both these varieties grow more slowly than the species, but all do better if trained up a moss-stick, so that their aerial roots can get a footing. With age the plants become straggly and the leaves are smaller. A good light is important to maintain the variegation, especially for the varieties, but avoid hot summer sun. Give plenty of water in summer, with some drying-out between waterings, and water sparingly in winter. Provide a MWT of 13°C (55°F), and ensure that the atmosphere is very humid.

Fittonia

Fittonias are mostly small creeping plants, found in Peru, whose oval leaves are covered in a network of coloured veins. In *F. argyroneura* the leaves are white-netted. A small, more easily grown version, with leaves 20 mm ($\frac{3}{4}$ in) rather than 5 cm (2 in) long, has the name 'Snakeskin'. *F. verschafffeltii* is also netted with veins, is pink instead of white, and its variety 'Pearcei' has red patterning.

A little shade and high humidity are important. The MWT should be 16°C (60°F), with average watering in summer and sparing amounts in winter. They make good undercover plants.

Glechoma hederacea 'Variegata' (syn. *Nepeta hederacea*, ground ivy)

The plain green-leaved form of this grows wild outdoors in Britain, but this variegated form is not quite so hardy. However, it is still easily grown, and ideal for hanging baskets, and for underplanting as groundcover, as it will root at each leaf-joint. The plant's toothed leaf edges are white, and the whole leaf is kidney-shaped and slightly aromatic. Small, light purple-blue flowers appear on the plant from spring until early summer.

It will grow in light shade, but a good

Fittonia argyroneura 'Snakeskin' has startling, white-netted veins.

Here is *Hedera canariensis* 'Maculata' doing what an ivy does best – climbing and twining to form a pretty shape.

The engagingly named freckle-face, or polka dot plant, needs lots of light to break out in bright pink spots.

light maintains the contrast between the green and white colouring; average summer temperatures and cool winter ones suit it best, down to a minimum of 4.5°C (40°F). Water plentifully in summer, but keep on the dry side without wilting, in winter; humidity can be average at all times. Cut back really hard in late winter or early spring, otherwise it becomes much too long and straggly.

Gynura sarmentosa (syn. *G. scandens*, purple velvet plant)

This is a delightful plant, whose leaves appear to be made from velvety purple plush, unique amongst plants grown in indoor gardening. It comes from high up on mountains in east Africa, where it grows in thin woodland, and from eastern Asia. As the plants mature, the stems become somewhat climbing, or they can be encouraged to grow trailing and hanging.

The leaves are more or less oval, with deeply toothed edges, and between 2.5–6.5 cm (1–2½ in) long. Small orange-red, daisy-like flowers appear in summer, best removed to maintain good foliage.

A good light is vital, with some sun, to ensure the intensity of the leaf colouring in the home; MWT should be 10°C (50°F), and the plant should be well watered from

spring to early autumn, sparingly for the rest of the year. Average humidity is sufficient; to keep the plant bushy rather than straggly, pinch out the tips of the shoots in spring and mid summer.

Hedera (ivy)

The pattern made by ivy leaves is so attractive that it is used widely for decorating china, on wrapping paper, furnishing fabrics, wall coverings, and other similar materials in daily use. But you can have the real thing as well if you grow your own ivy, and not necessarily in the standard plain dark green, but in attractively variegated leaves.

The small-leaved ivies are charming, especially 'Glacier' (a mixture of dark green, grey-green and creamy yellow); 'Jubilee' or 'Goldheart' (with a brilliant yellow centre to the leaves); 'Lutzii' (speckled light and dark green); 'Harald' (with white-edged leaves) and 'Buttercup' (young leaves and shoots all bright yellow). For a large-leaved ivy try the Canary island ivy 'Variegata' (syn. *H.* 'Gloire de Marengo'), with its grey-green marbling and white-edged leaves carried on red stems, a much bigger plant altogether.

Grow the ivies up supports such as trellises or canes; try the moss-poles so

that the aerial roots can find a foothold, and train them into various shapes, such as circles, triangles, or balls, with the help of wire frames. The small-leaved kinds make good trailers, too, for hangers and hanging baskets. The Canary island ivy will grow into a large, well-clothed plant several metres tall, and nearly as wide; the small-leaved kinds are slow growing.

Cool temperatures suit the ivies (which originate in Europe) best. Provide a MWT of 4.5°C (40°F), except for the Canary island ivy which needs 10°C (50°F); a moist atmosphere and moderate watering, though sparing in winter and a good light will keep them thriving and well-coloured. In hot, dry conditions greenfly and red spider mite will infest them.

Hypoestes phyllostachya (polka dot plant, freckle-face)

Often sold as *H. sanguinolenta*, the pretty polka dot plant breaks away from the cream, white or yellow variegations of many plant leaves, and produces bright pink spots and blotches on the leaf surface, particularly marked in the variety 'Splash'. It comes from Madagascar, and reaches a height of 15–30 cm (6–12 in).

As much light as possible is necessary to ensure the brightest spotting, though

High humidity and reasonable warmth are vital for marantas, distinguished by their prominent leaf markings.

Peperomia argyreia, or watermelon peperomia, is a lush-looking plant from the tropical rain forests in America. Its handsome, longways striped leaves command a second look.

avoid the midday sun in summer. Water well while growing, but sparingly in winter, and give average humidity and a MWT of 10°C (50°F). Pinch out the stem tips to keep it bushy, and prevent it from flowering. Watch for scale insect.

Maranta

In the same family as the calatheas, the Brazilian marantas have leaves with similar markings, though they are differently shaped, being oval rather than long, and are much smaller plants. The species *M. leuconeura* is the prayer plant, its name coming from the habit of raising its leaves at dusk so that they fold together like praying hands; *M. l. kerchoveana*, has brown blotches between the veins of the grey-green leaves, and is the most commonly seen and easiest to grow.

The herring-bone plant, *M. l. erythrophylla*, has red veins on the upper surface, and a light green mid-rib. *M. l. leuconeura* varies the colouring with white veins on a velvety olive-green background, and is the least easy to cultivate.

A high humidity is vital to prevent the thin leaves of the marantas withering at the edges. The MWT should be 16°C (60°F), with good warmth in summer; ensure a draught-free environment, a little shade in summer and good light in winter to maintain the colouring. Careful watering with soft water at room temperature is also important – never let the compost become dry.

Oplismenus hirtellus

In its native countries of tropical America and Africa, this grass must be a menace, as it has creeping stems which grow rapidly and root at each leaf joint. But as an indoor plant in hanging baskets, wall pots or hangers, it is ideal, being easily grown, colourful, and simplicity itself to increase.

'Variegatus' is the form usually grown, with narrow, sharply pointed leaves about 7.5 cm (3 in) long, striped in pink, white and green. If you want a change from tradescantia, try this comparatively recent introduction.

Average humidity, a good light, MWT of 7°C (44°F) and moderate summer watering, with sparing amounts in winter are all that it needs. Use the tips of shoots each spring for new plants, as the older ones are less colourful.

Peperomia

The peperomias are a large group of fleshy plants, mostly from the tropical rain-forests of America. Many are grown in containers, and three of the most commonly seen are *P. caperata* 'Variegata' – the rat-tail plant, *P. argyreia* – the watermelon peperomia, and *P. magnoliaefolia* 'Variegata'.

The first is quite a small plant, reaching a height of 15 cm (6 in). It has corrugated, dark green, heart-shaped leaves, edged creamy white, and narrow white flower spikes on pink stems from spring to winter. The second has handsome leaves, longitudinally banded in dark and silvery green stripes on a thick, slightly pointed, rounded leaf. It grows to 20 cm (8 in) high. And the third is a much more upright plant being 30 cm (12 in) tall, whose leaves can be almost completely creamy white, becoming pale green as they mature.

Besides these upright and bushy forms of peperomias, there are also some trailing varieties, not often seen, but good plants for growing in the home; as is characteristic of the other peperomias, they have fleshy leaves and stems.

Peperomia scandens 'Variegata' is a rather stiffly trailing kind, which can be trained to grow vertically – its stems will reach to between 60 and 90 cm (2 and 3 ft) long, on which there will be broadly and irregularly yellow-edged leaves carried alternately on the reddish stems.

If you can track down *P. prostrata*, you will have an altogether neater plant, with small leaves – 1.5 cm (½ in) wide – netted with white.

The fleshiness of the plants means that watering in summer should be moderate, decreasing to sparing in winter, though the compost should never dry out completely. They are not fussy about humidity, and the light should be good to shaded. Provide a MWT of about 13°C (55°F), with normal summer temperatures.

Pilea cadierei (aluminium plant)

The silvery white markings, on the surface of the pointed oval leaves of this small plant, are caused by air beneath the surface of the outer layer of leaf tissue forming bubbles and lifting the tissue. From the Vietnamese forests, the aluminium plant was introduced as a single plant in 1938, its cuttings being responsible for

most of those plants now grown in the home.

The size of this rounded plant is about 30 cm (12 in), with leaves reaching up to 7.5 cm (3 in) long. A newer dwarf form called 'Compacta' is half the size.

The leaves drop quickly with winter cold or soggy compost. Therefore supply a MWT of not less than 10°C (50°F), and water sparingly in winter, but freely in summer, allowing the compost to become dryish between watering. A good light, and some humidity are necessary.

Plectranthus oertendahlii (Swedish ivy)

Just refer to this as Swedish ivy – the botanic name is quite unpronounceable, as well as being impossible to spell! Nevertheless, it is one of the easiest and most attractive plants to grow. The white-veined, dark green leaves are reddish on the underside, growing on reddish stems from which pink tube-shaped flowers appear in summer. Grow it as a trailing plant, or plant it as ground cover for large plants.

This native of Natal, South Africa, is not

The leaves of *P. magnoliaefolia* 'Variegata' can be almost completely creamy white, becoming pale green as they mature.

A little shade and daily misting are among the requirements for the feathery-fronded table ferns.

Setcreasea purpurea's deep purple hue is maintained by a good light with some sun. Pinching out the tips of shoots prevents its tendency to straggle.

a demanding plant; it is indifferent to humidity, grows in a good light or a little shade, needs a MWT of 10°C (50°F), and accepts average watering.

Pteris

The table ferns, as the varieties of *P. cretica* are called, are quite small ferns from both temperate and tropical parts of the world. They reach about 30 cm (12 in) tall, more when well suited, the fronds being feathery and deeply cut, arching over at the tips, with wiry stems.

The species is plain green; *P. c.* 'Albolineata' is light green down the centre of each frond segment. A variety of another species, *P. ensiformis* 'Victoriae', has broader fronds, centred with silvery white.

Provide plenty of soft, lukewarm water while growing, less while resting, acid compost, and a MWT of 10°C (50°F) to prevent the ferns from dwindling away. A little shade, and frequent daily misting are also necessary.

Rhoeo spathacea (boat-lily)

The boat-lily is a Central American plant grown for the sake of its foliage; the pointed narrow leaves, 23 cm (9 in) long, are olive-green on the upper surface, purple below, and are arranged in an arching rosette on a short central stem.

There is a variety called *vittata* whose leaves are longitudinally striped with yellow on the olive-green upper side, and this contrast with the purple underside makes it a striking and handsome plant. Small

white flowers appear between late spring and midsummer, carried in purple bracts shaped like miniature boats on the lower part of the plant.

Cultivation is uncomplicated; a MWT of 10°C (50°F) is necessary, with a sparing amount of water and plenty of light at that season. In summer water normally, feed, provide a good light together with the prevailing summer temperatures, and remember that the boat lily likes a good deal of humidity as well.

Sansevieria (bowstring hemp)

The variety commonly grown in containers is *S. trifasciata* 'Laurentii', mother-in-law's-tongue, a plant with extraordinarily stiff, vertical leaves, thick and fleshy, ending in a sharp point. Banded light on dark green, they have bright yellow margins, and produce spikes of white, fragrant flowers in really warm environments.

S. hahnii is quite different in habit, consisting of a rosette of broad, fleshy leaves at ground level, also dark and light green banded. There is a variety called 'Golden Hahnii' with deep yellow leaf margins. All come from tropical west Africa, where the fibres in the leaves are woven into mats, hats, bow-strings, and many other everyday objects.

Supply average humidity, a good light or some shade, and moderate watering in summer, though very sparing in winter, more like that required for cacti. A MWT should be 10°C (50°F); wet compost and cold result in basal rot.

Saxifraga stolonifera (mother-of-thousands)

The family of the saxifrages is vast; practically all of them are hardy, and are found growing in mountainous regions. This Chinese version is not quite hardy, and has dark green, slightly hairy leaves, veined with white on the upper side and reddish on the underside. Mother-of-thousands has airy sprays of tiny white flowers in late spring–early summer, grows to about 30 cm (12 in) high, and produces long red creeping stems with plantlets on the end – they can either dangle down round the plant or lie along the compost and root into it.

There is an even more attractive, slightly smaller version, 'Tricolor', whose leaves are white-edged and pink-flushed.

Mother-of-thousands is easily grown with average humidity and watering, a good light or a little shade, and normal summer temperatures, dropping to a MWT of 2°C (35°F). 'Tricolor' is less easy, needing a MWT of 10°C (50°F), and careful watering, otherwise it rots at the base. Watch for red spider mite and greenfly on both plants.

Scindapsus see Epipremnum

Senecio macroglossus variegatus (wax vine, Cape ivy)

If you want to test your friends' knowledge of plants, ask them what this is and which plant family it belongs to. Most of them will immediately plump for ivy. But it actually belongs to the Daisy family, and is in no way related to ivy; it produces clusters of small yellow flowers like daisies in winter if provided with a good light and some sun.

The habit of growth is climbing, but not too fast, and the plant can be kept in check and rather bushy if the shoot tips are nipped back. The yellow-edged leaves are fleshy, and quite large – up to 6.5 cm (2½ in) long. The wax vine has the bonus of being easier to look after than ivy if growing in warmth and a dry atmosphere. Humidity is not an essential requirement, though an occasional overhead misting will clean the leaves and be of benefit to the plant. Water sparingly in winter, normally at other times, and provide a MWT of 10°C (50°F), together with average temperatures throughout the summer growing season.

Setcreasea purpurea (purple heart)
A foliage plant (native of Mexico) of a remarkable colour, the stems and long narrow leaves of this stiffly trailing plant being deep purple all year, with small, pink-purple flowers at the tips of shoots in summer. It grows profusely all year round in warmth, and is used for groundcover in tropical outdoor gardens. It makes an effective contrast when mixed with plain, green-leaved foliage plants.

Main requirement for a really deep purple is a good light with some sun; a MWT of 10°C (50°F) with normal summer warmth; water well in summer, moderately in winter, and supply average humidity. Pinching out the tips of shoots will keep it from straggling, and they can be used for cuttings, which root easily.

Syngonium podophyllum (goosefoot plant)
The common name refers to the shape of the adult leaves which are divided into three, and eventually seven or more, leaflets; while young they consist of one leaf-blade only.

Podophyllum comes from two Greek words: *podos* meaning a foot, and *phyllon*, a leaf. These central American plants are technically climbers, but very slow, and start as a cluster of long-stalked leaves, from the centre of which a main stem slowly emerges. The central leaf veins are white on a green background.

Plenty of humidity, a high MWT of 16°C (60°F), a good light, and only moderate watering in summer, with sparing amounts in winter, will keep it in good order. If a climbing habit seems to be developing, attach the plant's stem to a moss stick.

Tradescantia (wandering Jew)
Tradescantias (from South America) are nearly always the first plants grown by indoor gardeners; their trailing stems and striped leaves are decorative and well-suited to macramé hangers and containers hung on walls. They are also no trouble to grow!

T. fluminensis has slender growth and can be white or yellow-striped; the plain green form tends to flush pink if kept short of water. *T. albiflora* 'Albovittata' is altogether stouter and more robust, with grey-green leaves and much white striping. It

An intriguing change in leaf shape confers interest and name on the goosefoot plant.

can cover a hanging basket, making a complete ball of foliage and stems.

Good light will ensure good variegation. Feed during the growing season as they grow fast, and water well, but sparingly in winter. Provide a MWT of 7.5°C (45°F), together with average humidity. They are easy to increase by rooting the shoot tips; removing them from *T. fluminensis* will keep the plant from straggling.

Zebrina (wandering Jew)
A good example of why plants have a botanic name – it distinguishes plants, such as tradescantia and zebrina, which share the same common name, even though in this case there is no visual reason why this should be so. They look quite different.

Z. pendula is most attractive, having 5-cm (2-in) long leaves banded in silvery green, purple and dark green, stiffly trailing to about 30 cm (12 in) in a season. *Z. purpusii* is largely purple or purple-green, and *Z.* 'Quadricolor' is striped with dark green, silvery green, purple and rosy purple on the upper side, and shades of purple underneath. All have pinkish or lilac flowers late in the summer. The plant is a native of Mexico.

Particularly suitable where trailing plants are required, zebrinas will grow in a good light or a little shade, with moderate summer watering and sparing amounts of water in winter. The colour is better if the plant is kept slightly on the dry side. Provide average humidity and a MWT of 10°C (50°F).

SPECIAL-CARE PLANTS

The majority of plants grown in the home have much the same needs as regards compost, watering, light, humidity, and so on, but there are some groups of plants which have to be treated differently. None is difficult to grow, and they all have qualities – of shape, colour, flowers or use – which set them apart from the general container plants.

BROMELIADS

These are plants which have adapted themselves to dry conditions, where they receive little rain or nutrients. The forest bromeliads live high up on trees, obtaining small amounts of moisture and food through their roots from the rotting remains of leaves, and other vegetation, which have collected in the hollow where the tree forks, or a branch joins a trunk. They can also live purely as epiphytes on trees, when their roots anchor them firmly in place.

There are other bromeliads which live on the ground in the forest, which can have quite large root-systems if they are growing in soil; many live amongst stones.

Both kinds of bromeliad receive most of their water from rain and dew which runs down the leaves into the funnel formed in the centre of the leaf rosette. Dissolved in the water will probably be the remains of insects, partly providing the mineral nutrients the plants require. All the bromeliads are from South America.

Light:	in the home, a good light
Water:	use tepid soft water poured straight into the funnel, which should be kept full while actively growing, and half full when resting. Keep the compost just moist to the touch. Take care not to over-water
Humidity:	average, with occasional misting
Temperature:	varies according to kind; see the descriptive list which follows; high summer temperatures for flowering
Compost:	peat-based
Feeding:	liquid-feed occasionally during the growing period
Position:	in the air or high up, hanging in baskets, wall pots, on 'rafts', hangers, or on 'trees'

The urn plant's bright pink flowerhead lasts several months.

Aechmea fasciata (urn plant)

Aerial. Broad, strap-shaped leaves, grey green and silvery banded, about 45 cm (18 in) wide, forming a funnel-shaped rosette. The bright pink flowerhead, on a 38 cm

The boldly variegated forms of ananas are admirably showy, as is the plant's flower.

(15 in) stem, lasts several months; small, bright blue, tubular flowers appear in summer. The plant dies after flowering, but offsets at the base can be grown on. MWT 10°C (50°F). Give all light possible, and high summer temperatures to ensure flowering of new offsets.

Ananas (pineapple)
Terrestrial. Variegated forms are most attractive; *A. comosus* 'Variegatus' has narrow, green arching leaves, is edged creamy white and is sharply spined. It forms a funnel-centred rosette which can be nearly 1.2 m (4 ft) wide, but is usually less. *A. c.* 'Striatus' is similar, but the cream stripes are marked with pink. It can

produce small pink fruit in about three years (not edible), but needs a high temperature and humidity to do so. Protect from draughts; will tolerate dry air; grow in peaty compost and a container; provide a MWT of 10°C (50°F).

Billbergia nutans (angel's tears)
Terrestrial. Angel's tears has long, narrow, grey-green pointed leaves with small spines on the edges, arching from the centre to form a plant 39 cm (15 in) wide. Curious, dangling flowers coloured navy-blue, yellow, pink and green, emerge from pink sheaths in mid-late spring on stems 30 cm (12 in) tall.

Forms offsets at the base very readily,

and soon fills a 15-cm (6-in) pot. Extremely easy to grow, needs pot and compost rather than raft or bark. Provide a little shade and a MWT of 4.5°C (40°F).

Cryptanthus (earthstar)
Mainly terrestrial. *C. bivittatus* has 15–20-cm (6–8-in) wide, flat, leaves which are green, flushed pink, with cream stripes in good light; dark and light green striped in shade. *C. bromelioides* 'Tricolor', is an upright plant growing to 30 cm (1 ft) high, with 2.5-cm (1-in) wide leaves, striped creamy white and green, edged pink, and flushed pink in the centre. *C. fosterianus*, also upright, growing to at least 60 cm (2 ft) wide, banded with grey on reddish-

Angel's tears beautifully describe this plant's drooping flowers.

67

brown. Water the compost sparingly in winter, normally in summer; grow in containers of peat-based compost; MWT 10°C (50°F). Good light gives best colouring.

Neoregelia carolinae 'Tricolor'

Aerial. Narrow leaves, shiny – unusual for a bromeliad – arching from the central shallow funnel to form a plant about 45–60 cm (18–24 in) wide, centrally striped with cream and pink; youngest leaves in centre, bright red just before flowering; reddish purple flowerhead, rounded, just below water surface, flowers violet-blue just above surface appearing at intervals over many months.

N. spectabilis, the fingernail bromeliad has bright red leaf tips, silvery grey bands underneath; it is rather flat-growing, up to 60 cm (2 ft) wide. Bright blue flowers. Good light; dry air; MWT of 16°C (60°F).

Tillandsia (air plants)

Aerial. *T. lindeniana*, unusually, is grown mainly for flowering, as a flattened flowerhead. It is rose-coloured, about 15 cm (6 in) long, and 45 cm (18 in) wide. It has deep blue flowers protruding from it in summer; leaves are purplish beneath. Some recently introduced species include *T. ionantha*, 5 cm (2 in) tall, consisting of tufts of narrow, grey, arching leaves; *T. argentea*, similarly coloured with almost hair-like leaves; and *T. juncea*, with narrow and much longer, vertical leaves emerging from a central point, as do those of the other species.

These three must have a lot of humidity all year round as they absorb moisture only from the air, from which they obtain food also, using minute dust particles. Grow on pieces of bark or wood, not in compost. *T. lindeniana* needs high humidity also, and all need a MWT of 16°C (60°F).

Vriesea splendens (flaming sword)

Aerial. This is a handsome plant with a deep funnel, formed from green strap-like leaves, cross-banded with chocolate brown. Diameter is about 60 cm (2 ft); the flat flower spike is at least 30cm (1 ft) long, brilliant red, with yellow flowers appearing from mid to late summer. Needs high humidity; MWT 18°C (65°F).

Stripes or prominent bands are features of the earth star. Good light gives best colouring.

CACTI

The cactus tribe is an enormously varied collection of plants that are great fun to grow. Many are easy to flower, and extremely ornamental when they do so. Many, too, are fascinating to grow because of their bizarre and exotic shapes. Like the bromeliads, they have adapted their habits of growth and metabolism to dry areas, with the difference that a lot of them also live in extremely hot climates as well.

The round shape of many varieties ensures that they give off the least possible water vapour, because such a shape is one which has the smallest surface area for a given internal volume. They have a thick skin, with the internal tissue having gradually modified over countless centuries so that it will absorb much more liquid than plants growing in more conventional conditions. Roots, too, have adapted to infrequent heavy bursts of rain by spreading widely and shallowly so that they can absorb as much moisture as possible before it evaporates in the heat or drains away.

The most important point to remember about cacti and succulents is that they are living; just because they live mainly in desert areas does not mean that they do not need food or drink. On the contrary, they need as much while growing as do other plants, but unlike them they will suffer neglect for much longer periods without showing signs of distress. However, neglect certainly isn't good for them, and they will not develop into the interesting and ornamental plants that they can and should be without proper care.

Some cacti are known as forest cacti and, like the bromeliads, are epiphytes, perching on tree branches and forks. They are cultivated in exactly the same way, and carry some of the most beautiful flowers of all. For the needs of the forest cacti, see those described in the bromeliad section and *not* those given below. All cacti come from the Americas.

Light:	as much as possible, particularly in winter
Water:	water normally in spring and summer; about once a month in winter to keep the compost barely damp
Humidity:	not necessary

Interesting mounts are important to display airplants at their best.

Temperature:	normal summer ones, MWT 7.5°C (45°F), but see exceptions under individual descriptions
Compost:	proprietary cactus compost for best results, or peat-based mixtures, or soil-based John Innes with 1 part grit added to every 3 parts compost
Feeding:	liquid-feed between mid summer and autumn, with high-potash compound fertilizer

Aporocactus flagelliformis (rat-tail cactus)
Long, hanging cylindrical stems about 13 mm (½ in) thick; tubular cerise flowers appear in early spring along the stems.

Keep compost just moist in winter.

Cephalocereus senilis (old man cactus)
Forms a vertical column which in its native Mexican habitat grows to 12 m (40 ft), though plants of this height are very old ones. The column is covered in long white hairs which can be cleaned with shampoo. Allow compost to dry all winter; use cactus compost, or John Innes with two parts grit, not one; MWT of 4.5°C (40°F).

Chamaecereus silvestrii (peanut cactus)
A jolly little cactus with many short fat prostrate stems, 7.5 cm (3 in) long, which are easily knocked off and useful for increase. Red tubular flowers, funnel-shaped, opening to a wide, many-petalled mouth, 5 cm (2 in) wide, in late spring-early summer. Flowers easily and profusely if given plenty of light and kept dry and cold in winter with a MWT of 0°C (32°F).

Epiphyllum (waterlily or orchid cactus)
One of the most beautifully flowered of forest cacti; stems flattened and leaf-like; rather ungainly, averaging 45 cm (18 in) long; large, open, many-petalled flowers 7.5 cm (3 in) or more wide; many hybrids in pink, red, white, yellow, orange, appearing mid to late spring, sometimes also early autumn. Maximum light in winter; MWT of 10°C (50°F); support the stems.

Gymnocalycium mihanovichii 'Friedrichii'
The name is bigger than the plant! Grown for its bizarre appearance, which consists of a rounded, prominently ribbed stem looking like a segmented ball, coloured bright red, grafted on top of a short length of the winged stem of *Myrtillocactus geometrizans*. Height 7.5 cm (3 in); difficult to keep through winter due to basal rotting; keep slightly moist; maintain an MWT of 13°C (55°F).

The rat-tail cactus's cerise flowers appear in early spring.

The glorious flowers of the waterlily or orchid cactus are well worth waiting for. They sometimes appear in early autumn as well as in spring.

The range of colours is part of the attraction of epiphyllum's spectacular flowers.

Looking like exotic pompoms, mammillaria produce circlets of daisy-like flowers.

Mammillaria quickly form nests of spiny plant bodies filling the pot.

Lobivia

Easily grown cacti, rounded, gradually becoming columnar, readily producing offsets; varieties grown in pots reach up to 15 cm (6 in) tall; red or yellow funnel flowers open flat to a diameter of 5–10 cm (2–4 in) in early summer. Keep dry in winter; MWT of 0°C (32°F); extra good drainage.

Mammillaria

Literally hundreds of species, with entire books and societies devoted to them; many varieties flower easily. Usually completely round, 2.5–15 cm (1–6 in) tall, quickly forming nests of plant bodies filling the pot; young ones can be used for increase; open daisy-like flowers in circlet, grow on top of the plant, in all colours but blue or orange, during early summer-autumn. No water in winter; MWT of 7.5°C (44°F).

Opuntia (prickly pear, bunny ears)

The opuntias look quite different to other cacti. *O. ficus-indica* produces fruit, but is too large for home-growing; *O. microdasys albispina* (bunny ears) is a better choice –

Round, clustering rebutia flowers when only one year old.

the branched stems are flattened oval pads covered in tiny white barbed spines, slowly growing to 90 cm (3 ft) tall; *O. m. minima* is much shorter, at 30 cm (12 in).

Keep slightly moist in winter; MWT of 7.5°C (45°F), preferably higher.

Rebutia

These small, round, clustering cacti will flower when only one year old, and are easily grown from seed. *R. minuscula* is about 5 cm (2 in) tall and has red, funnel-shaped flowers in early summer almost as big as it is; *R. senilis* has long white spines and is also red-flowered; *R. pygmaea* is only 2.5 cm (1 in) tall and produces orange-red flowers.

There are many more worth growing. Keep almost completely dry in winter, with a MWT of 7.5°C (45°F); in summer they need some humidity.

Rhipsalidopsis gaertneri (Easter cactus)

The beautiful Easter cactus has flattened, leaf-like stems arching and hanging down, which freely produce bright red, fuchsia-like flowers with pointed petals in spring.

After flowering, stand the cactus outdoors in a slightly shaded place, when frost risk is past, bring it in during mid autumn and keep at 10°C (50°F); water it a little at this stage. From early winter increase watering and raise temperature to about 18°C (65°F), liquid-feed with a high-potash fertilizer when flowerbuds begin to appear until flowering finishes. Repot about every third year after flowering.

Schlumbergera × buckleyi (Christmas cactus)

The magenta, fuchsia-like double flowers of the Christmas cactus are profusely produced in early winter from leaf-like, jointed stems forming an arching plant, which grows to 60 cm (2 ft) wide and more.

Treat the Christmas cactus like the Easter cactus, but encourage it to rest from mid winter–mid spring with sparing watering and a temperature of 13°C (55°F). In early autumn bring the cactus indoors – the time of flowering can be delayed by keeping the temperature at 13–16°C (55–60°F), and lengthening each day with artificial light.

Rebutia covered in colourful, outsize flowers is a delightful sight.

The Christmas cactus produces a profusion of flowers, swept back as though poised for flight.

ORCHIDS

The orchids are a very special collection of flowering plants, the most advanced, botanically speaking, of the plants in a group called the monocotyledon, which also contains bulbs, grasses and reeds; they are probably the most advanced in development to date of any plants. The curious, lovely, and sometimes bizarre flowers of the orchids are always fascinating, often being strangely, as well as beautifully, coloured and patterned.

Although many orchids require special conditions for growing, which cannot be provided in the average home, there are some that are easily grown, though they do need slightly different handling to the majority of indoor plants.

Compost:	buy a special orchid compost, or make up one consisting of 3 parts osmunda fibre and 1 part sphagnum moss (by volume). Mix them thoroughly, then use the mixture moist, and at atmospheric temperature
Watering:	water well while growing, sparingly during winter and, whatever the season, allow to partially dry out between waterings. Use lukewarm, soft water
Light:	a good light spring and summer, but no sun; in autumn, plenty of sun to ripen the plants, with a good light and some sun in winter
Humidity:	plenty of humidity all year is essential
Temperature:	MWT generally no lower than 7.5°C (45°F); in summer, keep on the cool side, about 16–21°C (60–70°F), but can vary for individual species
Feeding:	liquid-feeding generally not necessary, but see descriptions
Potting:	this is usually necessary when the container is full of roots and pseudobulbs –

about every three years – but it varies according to species. Do it in spring, and remove dead roots, rotting compost, and soft brown bulbs. Put pieces of crock vertically in the base of the pot to half-fill it. Add a little compost on top, then put the plant into the pot so that the back of it is against the rim of the pot, and there is about 5 cm (2 in) clear space at the front of the plant. Work in more compost, between, under the roots if necessary, and on top, so that the plant sits just below the rim of the pot. Do not pack it in too firmly, otherwise the drainage will be poor, but ensure that it is firm enough for the plant to be held by the stems after potting without the pot falling away. Water, put in shade for several weeks

The common name, tiger orchid, conveys something of the powerful impact made by *Odontoglossum grande's* bizarrely patterned flowers.

The slipper orchid has a prominent, pouch-like lower petal.

A striking variety of the slipper orchid.

Coelogyne cristata

One of the most beautiful orchids to grow in the home, it has white flowers, centred with yellow, each about 10 cm (4 in) wide. In spring there are about eight on a hanging spike.

Water sparingly in winter, so that the compost is almost dry. Do not repot unless essential as it can take two years after disturbance before flowers are produced again. From Nepal.

Cymbidium

Often used for corsages, the 5-petalled flowers can be yellowish green, pink, or green and yellow in the hybrids suitable for indoor cultivation. Flowering is in winter. From south-east Asia.

Odontoglossum

A spectacularly flowered orchid, *O.grande* is called the tiger orchid with 15-cm (6-in) wide flowers, consisting of five narrow, yellow and chestnut petals, and a rounded yellow 'lip'. Flowering is in winter. MWT of 10°C (50°F). From Guatemala.

Paphiopedilum (cypripedium, slipper orchid)

A well-known orchid with a prominent, pouch-like petal below three long flat ones; the colours are very varied, mainly greenish yellow, brown, white and purple, in various combinations. *P. insigne* is the best known slipper orchid, flowering in winter. Prevent draughts and watch for scale insect. From Nepal and Assam.

Pleione (Himalayan or Indian crocus)

In spite of its common name, this is not a crocus, but an orchid. The pretty and unusual flowers consist of a white central trumpet with a frilled opening, spotted red or magenta in the throat, surrounded by a collar of narrow, pointed petals varying in colour depending on the species. In the case of the commonly grown pleione, *P. bulbocodioides* (syn *P. formosana*), the flowers are deep purple to pale magenta.

Pleione flowers between late winter and late spring, the leaves appearing after flowering has started. They die down in autumn, when the plant rests. At that time the pseudobulbs should be kept virtually dry until early spring, when sparing water can be given, and gradually increased as the leaves appear. The temperature while resting can drop to 4.5°C (40°F).

The compost should consist of 2 parts loam and 1 part sphagnum moss (by volume), or a peat-based compost with a little sphagnum moss added. Grow pleiones in half pots, and plant the pseudobulbs so that the top part, about one-third of their length is above the compost surface.

Some of the most useful of the culinary herbs can be grown in containers in the home.

HERBS

Some of the most useful of the culinary herbs can be grown successfully in containers in the home, or in conservatories, glassed-in porches, or similar light and sheltered areas. Protection of this kind enables some herbs that would die down outdoors to continue growing, or at least to remain evergreen, consequently providing fresh, aromatic herbs for much, if not all, of the year.

Practically all the herbs described in the following list not only pay for their living, but are ornamental as well, as they flower in spring or summer, or have foliage that is sufficiently attractive to merit growing for that reason alone, for instance, pineapple mint or purple basil.

Parsley produces a mass of foliage which will last through winter into the following summer. It needs a good light and frequent misting.

Basil (*Ocimum basilicum*)
A bushy annual herb from Assam with thin, green, aromatic leaves smelling of cloves, growing up to 10 cm (4 in) long and nearly as wide, on stems reaching up to 60 cm (2 ft) tall in containers, topped by spikes of tiny white flowers in late summer and autumn. The leaves are the part used in cooking. A purple-leaved form called 'Opal' has violet flowers; it grows less vigorously, and is also used in cooking.

Sow two or three seeds in a 5-cm (2-in) pot in a temperature of 16–18°C (60–65°F) during mid spring, and barely cover with compost. Thin to one per pot, when large enough to handle, and pot into a 7.5-cm (3-in) and 13-cm (5-in) pot successively. Pinch out the tip of the stems at the third pair of leaves, and remove flower spikes to encourage leafiness and bushiness.

Keep in a good light with some sun, at normal summer temperatures; water freely and mist daily.

Bay (*Laurus nobilis*)
An evergreen shrub or small tree from the Mediterranean region. The aromatic, leathery leaves are used to flavour meat and fish dishes.

It can be kept quite small in a container by clipping once a year. The small yellow flowers appear in late spring. Water moderately, supply normal summer temperatures and humidity, with a MWT of 4.5°C (40°F), and give as good a light as possible, with sun. Clip to shape in late summer as a ball, pyramid or cone. Repot in alternate springs; watch for scale insect.

Chives (*Allium schoenoprasum*)
The grass-like leaves of chives (which originate in cool, temperate Europe) are tubular, and have a mild flavour of onions, making them very good for salads, dressings, dips and sandwiches. Can reach a height of 23–30 cm (9–12 in), but in containers is more likely to be about 15 cm

(6 in). In early summer, round lilac-pink flowerheads appear, lasting several weeks.

Grow from seed sown in normal temperatures in spring, putting several seeds in a 5-cm (2-in) pot. Pot on to 7.5 and 10-cm (3 and 4-in) pots as they grow. They do best in very well-drained compost, like cactus compost, with plenty of sun, moderate watering and average humidity and summer temperatures. The MWT can be down to freezing.

Marjoram, sweet (*Origanum onites*)
Sweet marjoram is an annual variety of marjoram easily grown in containers. Its soft grey-green leaves are delicately and spicily aromatic, good for rice, pasta and mushroom dishes in particular, as well as salads and chicken recipes. In early summer it has small, round, green buds from which very tiny white flowers appear.

Sow seeds in small pots in 18°C (65°F), and thin to the strongest in each. Give a good light with some sun, normal summer temperatures and humidity, and water moderately. Remove flower spikes to encourage leaf growth. From Asia and the warmer parts of Europe.

Mint (*Mentha × spicata*)
Garden mint is best grown in a container, even outdoors, to prevent it invading other plants. The roots – really creeping underground stems – send up shoots from each leaf-joint, about 23–45 cm (9–18 in) tall.

Besides garden mint, there are several others easily grown, including pineapple mint with soft, white-edged leaves, and ginger mint, yellow-variegated, both much less tall-growing; also consider eau de Cologne mint, with purple-flushed, dark green leaves and stems.

Water normally, and provide a good light with sun and average humidity and summer temperatures. The MWT can drop to freezing.

Parsley (*Petroselinum crispum*)
Parsley needs more room than it is usually given to grow to its full size, and accommodate the fleshy white tap-root. It produces a mass of foliage which will last through winter into the following summer.

Sow seed in 18°C (65°F) in 5-cm (2-in) pots in mid spring, thin to one per pot, and move into a 10-cm (4-in), and then a 13-cm (5-in) pot as it grows. Give a good light, water well and mist frequently, especially if kept in a room with central heating, as parsley likes to be cool, moist and in shade during part of the day.

The MWT can be 4.5°C (40°F), with normal warmth in summer. In the second summer it will flower and die. From northern and central Europe.

Rosemary (*Rosmarinus officinalis*)
Another Mediterranean inhabitant, rosemary is an evergreen shrub which, like bay, can be kept small in a container and clipped every year. Its narrow, grey-green leaves reach only 2.5 cm (1 in) in length, cover the stems, and produce small, tubular, pale-blue flowers in late spring, on spikes at the end of the stems.

Rosemary provides a favourite flavouring for lamb, chicken and pork dishes; in addition, it makes delicious sweet biscuits and, added to apple, supplies an unexpectedly peppermint flavour.

Water moderately in summer, sparingly in winter, give a good light with sun, and normal summer temperatures and humidity. The MWT can be 4.5°C (40°F). Clip in late summer.

Tarragon (*Artemisia dracunculus*)
The narrow green leaves are aromatically and deliciously spicy, reminiscent of cloves, but with delicate overtones peculiar to tarragon. They clothe a plant up to 60 cm (2 ft) tall outdoors, less in a container, and are used with lamb, chicken, tomatoes and mushrooms in particular, as well as a variety of savoury dishes. The French form is the one to use, being less vigorous than the Russian kind, which has a poor flavour.

Pot up small plants in spring – seed is not available – and use a well-drained compost. Supply a good light with sun, normal watering and humidity, summer warmth, and keep cool in winter at about 7.5°C (45°F). If it is too warm it will produce new shoots and exhaust itself. Divide after about three years of potting on.

Thyme (*Thymus vulgaris*)
As with the mints, there are many thymes, with many flavours. Common thyme has tiny green, evergreen leaves covering a dwarf shrub about 20 cm (8 in) tall, and rather more wide. Its strongly aromatic leaves are used a great deal in meat dishes,

particularly with lamb in southern Europe, its native home. In mid summer it produces masses of tiny lilac-pink flowers. Lemon thyme (*T.* × *citriodorus*) has lemon-flavoured leaves.

All thymes like plenty of sun and warmth, very good drainage, moderate watering and average or little humidity. In winter they can be kept on the dry side, but not too dry, otherwise the leaves fall. Requires a MWT of 4.5°C (40°F). Branches pegged down on to the compost will root.

Winter savory (*Satureja montana*)
An unusual, small, evergreen shrub from the eastern Mediterranean area. It grows only to about 23 cm (9 in) tall in a container, but has many stems. The green leaves look rather like those of rosemary, but are spicily hot, and add considerable flavour to dishes containing any sort of beans, salads, mushrooms and eggs. It has small white flowers in mid to late summer.

Give it the same conditions as rosemary: warmth, light and sun, good drainage, and moderate watering and humidity. In winter water sparingly, and give a MWT of 7.5°C (45°F).

CARING FOR INDOOR PLANTS

Some indoor plants require only the most basic attention – watering every few days, and cutting pieces off when they get too large. If you are completely inexperienced, and have always tended plants that require no more attention than the scanty amount described, it can come as quite a surprise when you buy different varieties which don't respond to such treatment. Either they die at once or lose most of their leaves or flowers.

The chances are that, if this happens, you have got hold of plants that need more time, attention, and knowledge of indoor gardening. Nonetheless, they are still very easy to grow.

Growing plants successfully in the home demands a sharp eye which picks up small changes in the plants, and an awareness that they are constantly altering from day to day. In time, just a swift glance over your plant collection will be enough to tell you whether all is well, but to start with it pays to look at them individually each day in more detail. In this way you will quickly spot even a small outbreak of greenfly or scale insect, a discolouring leaf, a few fallen flowers, compost beginning to dry out, and so on, before any of these features turn into major disasters.

This chapter deals in detail with each of the needs of indoor plants, and the reasons why they are important, and reveals how you can satisfy their requirements. The time you devote to your plants is up to you, depending on the number you have and how easy they are to grow. Whatever happens, don't lose sight of the fact that indoor gardening is a hobby, and should be fun – the advice given here is only a guideline, and there is no need to stick rigidly to it. Gardening is one subject above all in which there are as many opinions as there are gardeners!

CLIMATIC CARE

When you grow plants indoors you have complete control over three of their most important needs: temperature, humidity and water, together with some control over light. All these would depend on the climate in their natural habitat, modified by the weather from day to day, but in the home the plants will be solely dependant on you for the quality and quantity of these vital factors.

Temperature and humidity

Temperature and humidity go hand in hand. For most plants, the higher the temperature the more moisture in the atmosphere is needed.

Many indoor plants come from tropical countries near the equator, where the humidity is much greater than it is in the cooler areas of, say, northern Europe or north America.

Temperatures in summer are not a problem, as most indoor plants are satisfied with normal summer temperatures. A few like to be on the cool side, that is 16–18°C (60–65°F) in summer, and where this

Standing plants on gravel in a tray containing water ensures adequate humidity.

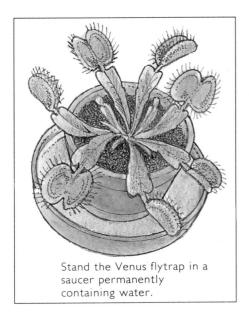

Stand the Venus flytrap in a saucer permanently containing water.

is so it is noted under individual plants in the descriptions. The minimum winter temperature that is acceptable is about 4.5–7.5°C (40–45°F); 2–5°C (5–8°F) above this will, however, produce a happier plant, while still ensuring that it has a winter rest. However, too high a temperature in winter can result in forced growth, which will in any case be weak because of the prevailing bad light.

Humidity is vital to prevent browning of leaf edges and tips, early falling of leaves, flowers and flower buds, and the infestation of greenfly or red spider mite. Plant foliage gives off water vapour constantly, but more slowly when the air is already moist, so there is much less stress on the plant. Unfortunately, for plants, the average home is not usually damp enough, especially when centrally heated, and is even drier if double-glazed.

To counteract this, you can mist the plant's top growth once or more times a day with ordinary soft water in a hand mister. You can also stand the plant on pebbles or gravel in a saucer or tray containing water, so that it is constantly evaporating around it. You can even put the plant's container in a larger one, and pack moist peat in the space between the two. Another method involves putting a shallow container of water near the plants, or using humidifiers by radiators. An even simpler method is to grow the plants in groups, so that they can create their own local humid atmosphere.

Watering

The higher the temperature the more the plants lose water through their leaves, and the more they need to absorb moisture from the compost. Water is therefore needed more often in hot weather, when plants are usually growing; if they are resting, as they generally do in winter, they will need much less. Note, however, that watering is not a matter of once a week, same day, same time. It is done when the plant needs it.

You can tell when a plant needs watering by the state of the compost surface. If it has become dry, you should water, using water at room temperature or a little warmer, and soft if you can manage it. In hard water areas use rain water, or let the mains water stand a day or two before use, or boil it and use when it has cooled. Give enough water to fill the space between the compost surface and the container rim; if none of this drains through, give the same amount again, and empty the surplus out of the saucer after about 20 minutes. All plants should stand in a pot-saucer or drip-tray to contain the inevitable dampness produced at the base of a container, particularly by plants growing in clay pots.

Plants which need plenty of water will need to be watered daily while growing, and probably with two doses rather than the normal one; moderate amounts will mean watering roughly every 4–10 days. Sparing watering will apply to plants which are resting, when watering every two to four weeks is all that is needed, just enough to keep the compost moist and prevent the roots from drying out completely.

Light

Another factor besides temperature which affects watering is the light the plants receive. In good light they will grow faster than in dull light, though some do better in shade. However, in the home there is one big drawback – there is no overhead light. Fortunately, though, modern windows do allow sufficient light in to grow a great number of foliage plants, and nurserymen have found many flowering plants which will also grow in these conditions.

The majority will grow in a 'good light' – a position near to a west- south- or east-facing window, but not necessarily in the sun. Indeed, midday summer sun shining through a window is too hot for all except geraniums, cacti, and one or two other species. Those plants which need a 'little shade' can be grown several paces away from the window, and some that will grow in 'shade' will grow in the furthest corners away from the light. However, in winter they need all the light they can get, including what sun there is, though you need to be careful with cyclamen, azaleas, and some other winter-flowerers.

PLANT CULTIVATION

Feeding

Plants are like any other living organism: they need fuel to supply the energy which drives their metabolism. This fuel comes in the form of mineral nutrients, plant foods which are absorbed through the roots as microscopic particles present in the soil water. These minerals include phosphorus, nitrogen and potassium – nitrogen is a gas, present in a chemically modified form as a solid. These three minerals are of major importance because they encourage root, leaf, and flower/fruit growth respectively. However, plants also need many other minerals, each required for different functions.

The modern proprietary composts contain these plant foods in varying amounts, depending on the brand of compost. Some composts contain sufficient foods to last the plant for the whole growing season, while others need to be topped up, preferably with a liquid fertilizer. These can consist of concentrates which must be diluted with water as the makers instruct, or of solutions which are ready to use, or of powders which are dissolved in water.

There is a variety of houseplant fertilizers available, and you should choose the one which is suitable for your group of plants. Foliage plants need plenty of nitrogen; flowering kinds need potassium; African violets phosphorus. The fertilizer container will always have a note on it detailing the nutrient content, and the amount and ratio of these elements.

Feeding depends on the type of compost. If using peat-based kinds, feeding is usually necessary from early summer to autumn, stopping when the growth slows down and the leaves begin to change

Modern windows allow in sufficient light to grow a great number of foliage and flowering plants.

colour. Feed about once a week. However, note that some winter-flowering plants are fed from the time the buds show until flowering stops, that others are fed when flowering finishes until they die down, and that some plants don't need feeding at all!

Grooming

To keep your plants looking their best, you should regularly groom and dust them. There will always be flowers and leaves discolouring and dying in the natural course of events, and removing them when they change colour not only maintains the plant's decorativeness, but also stops disease infecting the healthy plant through the decaying tissue.

Leaves should be cleaned gently with a moist sponge or soft cloth to show off their colouring, and ensure that they function properly. You can polish them, too, with a proprietary solution, which sometimes also contains nutrient and pesticide. 'Hairy' leaves, such as those of some of the foliage begonias, or of the African violet, should be cleaned with a soft brush.

Training

The taller plants, the climbers and the trailers will need tying to supports and training to fill their space evenly, so that they don't flop unceremoniously all over the place.

Tall plants grow better with their stems spaced out and attached to canes or trellises; climbers with aerial roots will need moss-poles, and it is essential that the moss is kept moist so that the plant's roots can attach themselves to it and absorb water. In this way, the whole plant will grow better. Climbers can be trained into various shapes, as can some of the non-climbers, such as the variegated lemon scented geranium, and the fuchsias.

Controlling a plant's shape

In outdoor gardening, quite a lot of regular and formal cutting and pruning is often required to shape roses, shrubs, and fruit trees so that they flower and fruit to their maximum. As far as indoor gardening is concerned most of this can be dispensed with, but it does pay to do a little discreet

nipping back to control exuberant climbers, and to keep the shape of the plants as symmetrical as possible, as well as encouraging flower production.

A lot of the flowering plants will flower magnificently if you pinch back the tips of the new sideshoots. This involves nipping out the tip of a shoot between finger and thumb, just above a leaf joint or pair of leaves, while the shoot is still young and growing. It should already have about three leaf joints on it; you remove the shoot above the third joint before it fully develops another leaf or pair of leaves.

New sideshoots will subsequently appear at each of the remaining leaf-joints, and because they will eventually carry flowers, the whole plant will bloom that much better. It will, however, flower slightly later, so if you want earlier flowering for any particular reason, don't pinch back. The pinching-back technique is usually carried out in late spring, and works especially well with fuchsias and busy lizzies.

If any shoots are growing much longer

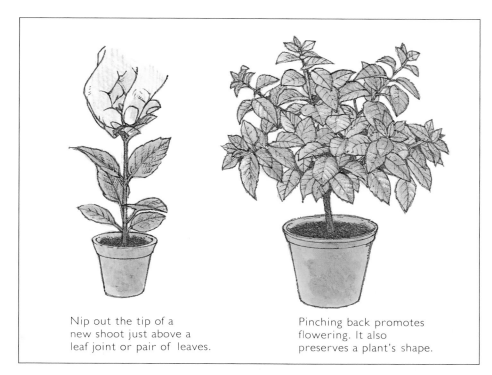

Nip out the tip of a new shoot just above a leaf joint or pair of leaves.

Pinching back promotes flowering. It also preserves a plant's shape.

Hibiscus, fuchsia, jasmine, and pelargoniums need to have their new growth of the previous season cut back by about half or one-third, and the tree-like foliage plants – fatsia, grevillea, and schefflera – may also need pruning. Always cut cleanly, and always make the cut just above a bud or leaf-joint. If the plant flowers in spring prune immediately after flowering, as next year's flowers will be produced on this year's new shoots.

Roots and their needs

As has already been mentioned, plants need fuel and water as do humans and animals. Since this need increases until a plant reaches maturity, its roots and top growth continually need more space, food, light, air, and water. While the liquid feeding referred to on page 81 will satisfy its needs for a while, there comes a time when it will be essential either to move the plant into a larger container, or supply it with much more food, or both.

Changing the container is referred to as potting on, because originally plants were grown only in pots – hence, putting them into one came to be known as potting, and moving them into a larger pot is called potting on. Although plants are now grown in all sorts of containers, the process is still called potting or potting on.

Plants which are growing steadily will only need to be potted on in early spring when growth is starting. Fast-growing varieties will need potting on once, or even twice during the growing season. Slow-growing kinds can be left alone for two or three years, and some plants actually

than the majority, pinching back can be done at any time during the growing season to bring them into line with the others, rather than to encourage flowering. This will preserve the plant's shape.

You can apply the same process to the leading shoots, the ones which form the main stem or trunk of the plant, to stop them getting too tall. Simply remove the tip at the height you want the plant to be, or a little below it, as it will grow a little more, and in any case the topmost sideshoots will grow quite long and attempt to continue the vertical growth.

When climbers are stopped in this way, by halting both the leading shoots and sideshoots, you will encourage a bushy rather than a climbing habit. Using the same technique, trailing plants can be prevented from getting straggly. Some can even be scissored back, such as the hearts-entangled (ceropegia), without any harm.

Pruning

If pruning has to be done, the best time is usually late winter or early spring, when the plant is about to start growing, and potting takes place.

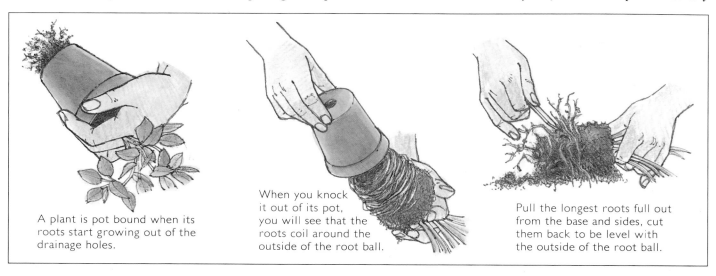

A plant is pot bound when its roots start growing out of the drainage holes.

When you knock it out of its pot, you will see that the roots coil around the outside of the root ball.

Pull the longest roots full out from the base and sides, cut them back to be level with the outside of the root ball.

flower better when the container is crammed tight with roots. Normally, though, plants should be potted on long before they reach this stage, when the roots have just reached the outside of the compost.

Compost
Besides more space, the roots will need more food. Since the growing medium, or compost, in which they are contained has a limited supply of plant nutrient, it will become necessary to replace this because, surprisingly, the compost itself gradually dwindles, and the roots become too compressed and short of air to survive, even with the liquid feeding.

Compost is used because the food content, drainage and oxygenating qualities of garden soil are unsuitable for container plants. The compost is a specially made-up – or composed – mixture, containing either peat, sand, chalk and nutrient, or all these ingredients plus specially selected good soil. The composts containing peat consist mostly of peat, and those with soil in them are largely soil. These soil-based kinds are called John Innes potting composts, and come in three grades: 1, 2 and 3, depending on whether they have twice as much or three times as much nutrient and chalk as the standard No 1.

Plants in pots up to a 10 cm (4 in) diameter size can grow in No 1; those in 10–18 cm (4–7 in) pots should have No 2;

and plants in larger diameter containers should be grown in No 3.

Peat-based composts are not graded in the same way. The proprietary brands vary in their nutrient content, and instructions for feeding and potting will be on the packet or sack. If you are growing plants which like what are called acid soils, use a compost called 'ericaceous' – azaleas and ferns need this kind to grow healthily.

Potting on
When potting on prepare a pot or other container, about 13–20 mm ($\frac{1}{2}$–$\frac{3}{4}$ in) larger in diameter, by putting a little moist compost into the base and firming it lightly in. If using a clay pot, put two or three crocks (broken pieces of clay pot or brick) curved side upwards in the bottom, underneath the compost. Ensure that the compost of the plant to be moved is moist all the way through.

Remove the plant from its existing pot by putting the fingers of one hand across the compost surface, turning it upside down with the other hand, and tapping the rim on the work surface – the plant should easily slide out of its container. Cut back any really long roots level with the rootball, and remove a little of the surface compost. Position the plant centrally in its new container, fill in compost around the sides, and firm it in with the fingers, until it is firm and level up to within 13 mm–5 cm ($\frac{1}{2}$–2 in) of the rim, depending on the size of the plant. This space is left for watering.

Finally, tap the container lightly on the work surface to settle the compost, water the plant well, let it drain, and put it in warm shade for a few days to settle down.

Potting large plants
If you are potting into the same size container in order to prevent the plant from getting larger, cut the rootball back at the sides and the base with a sharp knife to reduce it by about a quarter to a fifth. This will allow new compost to be added, and is useful where plants have grown really large. With such plants, you will often need a helper to hold the plant while you carefully remove the container.

Potting bulbs
If you are dealing with bulbs or corms it is usual to let them die down naturally after flowering, dry off and rest, and then repot them in the same size container, or one only a little larger, but with completely fresh compost. The old compost is discarded, and the withered roots are removed, but if new white ones have already started to appear, the old roots should only be partially removed, to avoid damaging the new ones.

PLANT HEALTH AND SICKNESS

Most of the troubles that occur on indoor plants are due to their being treated in the wrong way – not enough or too much light,

Repot a plant when its roots have filled the pot. Remove it carefully, trying not to disturb the root ball.

Place a little fresh compost in a new, larger pot, then stand the plant in it. Fill in around the roots with more compost.

Firm with the tips of the fingers, gently if the compost is peat based.

dry atmosphere, too low a temperature and, above all, the wrong quantities of water. The wrong treatment will result in discoloured, weak or dying plants, and in this state they are much more likely to be infested with pests or diseases, which will then finish them off. The pests and fungal diseases most likely to infect your plants are described below; under each heading are given details of the symptoms, the appearance of the pest or disease where appropriate, and the methods of dealing with it. The secret of success is therefore to give your plants the right growing conditions, whereupon your main problem will be to avoid being taken over by them! If you have to resort to the use of pesticides of any kind, always read the instructions beforehand, then follow them exactly when using the pesticide.

PESTS

Greenfly (aphids)
These are tiny green creatures up to 3 mm ($\frac{1}{8}$ in) long, sometimes winged, and they can occur in such numbers that they are sometimes called plant lice. They feed by sucking the sap from a leaf or stem through mouthparts which are rather like a hypodermic needle, which they use to stab the plant tissue. As a result the attacked areas become discoloured light green or yellow, curled and distorted, and stunted. The whole plant is weakened, and may easily be killed in a bad infestation. The greenfly congregate on the tips of shoots and the underside of leaves, mainly the youngest, and breed extremely fast.

This is where your daily inspection is most useful; if you spot one greenfly, there will certainly be ten more hidden, and you can deal with them at once with finger and thumb. If you have missed them, and a shoot is badly infected, remove it altogether by nipping it back to clean growth.

If a whole plant is infested, use a houseplant insecticidal spray containing permethrin, which is safe and effective – it is like pyrethrum, but even safer and much stronger.

Leafminer
A minute maggot which lives and feeds beneath the surface tissue of leaves, and makes tunnels, visible as twisting white lines on the leaf surface. Cinerarias and chrysanthemums are prone to this pest, but other plants can also be invaded. Remove complete leaves where infected, and spray the remainder on both surfaces wih malathion.

Mealybug
Similar to scale insect (see below) in its lifestyle and appearance, but the pest itself is covered with blobs of protective white fluff. Bulbs are its favourite host, particularly the amaryllis (hippeastrum), and it congregates at the neck of the bulb between the leaves. The young do not have fluff, and look like small, flattened, pale brown or yellowish discs, easily missed on leaves or stems. Remove carefully with a pointed knife, or paint with methylated spirits; a strongly pressured spray, containing malathion, to penetrate the fluff, can also be used.

Red spider mite
A sap-sucking pest like greenfly, but even smaller; you will need a hand-lens to see the pinkish, red or straw-coloured mites clearly on the underside of the leaf. What looks like white mites mixed with them are their cast skins. In bad attacks webbing will be present. Leaves become speckled greyish or yellowish, wither and brown, and then fall off. Plants can be killed if the infestation is allowed to continue unchecked.

Dry air and high temperatures encourage the mites to breed, as does insufficiently watered compost. Keep your plants well supplied with humidity and water, and in moderately warm temperatures rather than high ones, and they should remain free. Be very careful when you buy plants, to make sure the mites are not already present. Where there is an infestation, isolate the plant, remove badly affected parts, improve humidity and watering, and spray thoroughly with malathion, or use a systemic insecticide in the compost.

Scale insect
Another sap-sucker, this pest lives on the underside of leaves, along the main vein, or on the bark or stems of the main trunk. It is brown, grey or black, roughly round or oval, and about 3 mm ($\frac{1}{8}$ in) wide; the scale insect stays in the same place all its life while it feeds. When young, the scales are small and pale green.

Infested plants become weak, slow-

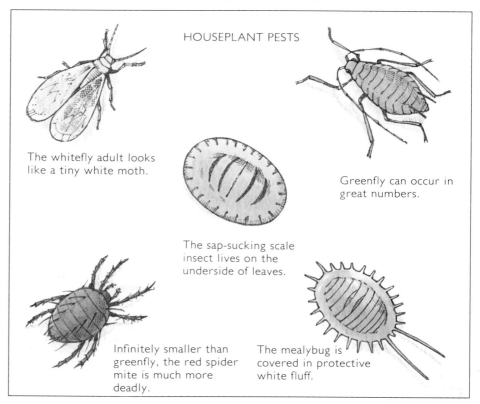

HOUSEPLANT PESTS

The whitefly adult looks like a tiny white moth.

Greenfly can occur in great numbers.

The sap-sucking scale insect lives on the underside of leaves.

Infinitely smaller than greenfly, the red spider mite is much more deadly.

The mealybug is covered in protective white fluff.

growing and stunted, as well as being covered in a sticky substance – the 'honeydew' that these pests excrete. Citrus, ferns, *Ficus benjamina* and sweet bay can be badly infested, and the tree-like pot plants in general are prone to invasion. Scrape the pests off gently with finger-nails, sponge off the stickiness, and give the whole plant a good wash all over with clear water sprayed on freely; then spray with malathion and repeat twice at the intervals the makers instruct.

Whitefly

This pest has two obvious stages, the whitefly adults which look like tiny white moths on the underside of the leaves, and the pale green to transparent scales or young, which do the damage by sap-sucking. Their worst effect is the copious quantity of sticky honeydew which is produced, making plants thoroughly unpleasant to handle, as well as weakening and distorting them. Fuchsias are very popular with this insect!

Removal of badly infested leaves and stems, and spraying at three- to four-day intervals with permethrin, which will kill the young as well as the adults, should eradicate an attack.

FUNGAL DISEASES

Grey mould

Universal, affecting all plants. It takes the form of a grey furry growth on leaves, stems and other plant parts, in spots and patches, preceded by browning of the tissue. Infected parts turn yellow, rot and fall off, and the disease spreads rapidly in conditions which are too cool and moist for the plant. Give more warmth, free the plant

of diseased growth, and spray the remaining parts with a systemic fungicidal solution of benomyl.

Mildew

Symptoms are powdery patches of white on leaves and stems; buds and flowers can also be infected, and the flowers may be discoloured as well as covered in white powder. The disease spreads rapidly when plants are dry at the roots and the atmosphere is moist and rather warm. Begonias can be badly infected, as can chrysanthemums.

Remove affected tissue carefully so as not to shake any fungal spores on to healthy tissue, and then spray the plant thoroughly with benomyl.

Sooty mould

Black patches on leaves and stems are evidence of this minor fungus disease. They will be found growing on the surface of the sticky honeydew produced by the feeding of scale insect, greenfly, mealy bug and whitefly and, although the fungus does not live as a parasite on the plant itself, it effectively blocks the breathing pores even more than the honeydew. However, the remedy is easy and simple: gently sponge it off the leaves, with clean water, and then spray if necessary with an insecticidal spray.

Azalea gall

Occasionally found on pot-grown azaleas, this fungus makes the leaves thick and discoloured grey-white with a bloom on the surface; sometimes flowers are also infected, when they lose their colour and become a sickly creamy white. Hand removal of affected parts as soon as seen should keep the disease under control.

Cultivation disorders

If none of the above seems to be the cause of a particular problem, then it is likely to be due to the fact that the plant is not being cared for correctly. The supply of the right quantity of water, warmth, humidity, light and food, and the size of container and type of compost are all factors which need to be right to ensure that a plant is healthy. If one or more of these is not exactly adjusted to a plant's needs, it will become sick.

Yellowing leaves. Slow change of colour, followed by falling, can be due to natural ageing, lack of the nutrient nitrogen, or overwatering; in the case of a rapid change of colour, the cause is likely to be sudden cold, or a sudden drop in temperature from the normal one. Change of colour in tip or youngest leaves, due to lack of nutrient iron, can occur if a plant is being grown in alkaline compost when it needs acid conditions. or being watered with hard instead of soft water.

Brown markings. If they are spots, these can be due to cold, poorly structured compost leading to poor drainage, dry fertilizer on leaves, too much food, or the sun shining through drops of water on the leaves. Brown edges and leaf tips are caused by dry atmosphere, draughts, shortage of the nutrient potassium (rare), or lime in the compost. Brown patches which are large and pale in colour, are due to sun scald. Fleshy leaves which turn brown at soil level and rot, result from wet compost and/or low temperature.

Wilting leaves/whole plant. The causes can be too little water, too much water, root aphids, too high a temperature.

Fading leaves. Lack of light is the reason for coloured leaves losing colour, or variegated yellow or white leaves becoming plain green. With variegations, if one shoot or branch only loses variegation, it is reverting, and should be cut off back to normally coloured growth.

Green leaves becoming pale and eventually a sickly brownish yellow are the result of too much light, characteristic of climbing foliage plants.

White marks on leaves. Cold water, or water that is not at room temperature applied to compost, or cold water on leaves are causes of white marks appearing on leaves.

Flowers, buds and/or fruit falling. Dry atmosphere, draughts, cold, too much or

The spread of grey mould on plants can be arrested by freeing the plant of diseased growth.

not enough water, moving the plant, turning it away from the light, or watering with cold water, are reasons for falling flowers, buds or fruit.

No flowers at all. The possible explanations for this condition are too much nitrogen, not enough light, warmth or potassium.

No fruit. Dry atmosphere, dry compost, lack of potassium can be factors in absence of fruit.

Badly shaped fruit. Dry air at pollination or fertilization time produces badly shaped fruits.

NEW PLANTS

Part of the fun of indoor gardening is obtaining new varieties to add to the collection. You may also want to increase your particular stock of plants because some are especially ornamental, or because you think they would make excellent presents, or could be used to supply a local charitable event.

In any case it is enjoyable to test your gardening skills, and if you are successful in multiplying your plants, you will find that it is one of the most satisfying aspects of gardening.

There are all sorts of different ways in which plants can be increased, some of them absurdly easy, since the plants have virtually done it for you. Those methods which are most appropriate to indoor gardening are described on the following pages, starting with the least difficult.

Plantlets

Some of the easiest to duplicate are those that provide ready-made replicas of themselves, such as mother-of-thousands (*Saxifraga stolonifera*), the spider plant (chlorophytum), the piggy-back plant (*Tolmiea menziesii*), and the urn plant (aechmea). All you have to do is detach the plantlets, and plant them in 5-cm (2-in) pots of compost; some of them will already have produced roots.

Division

This is another easy method of propagation which can be used, for example, on the Cape primroses, the Italian bellflower, rhizomatous begonias, *Sedum sieboldii*, and the cyperus.

It is easy to see which plants can be increased in this way because they may well have already produced new sections of the main plant, which are virtually whole new plants.

Removing and planting bulb offsets is also a kind of division. These offsets are smaller bulbs produced at the base of the old ones. Some plants produce tiny bulbs (bulbils) on the stems, such as the hearts-entangled plant (ceropegia).

This form of propagation should be carried out in the spring, or whenever you are repotting.

Seed

Annuals have to be grown from seed, sown in late winter-early spring, in a temperature of about 18°C (65°F), using proprietary seed-sowing compost. Sow the seeds in a quarter seed-tray, that is, a seed tray a quarter the size of the normal ones, or use a half-pot. Or try the proprietary compressed peat discs, which swell with water absorption to form a peat cylinder about 5.6 cm (2¼ in) tall, and a little narrower, or use small, 5-cm (2-in) pots.

Fill the container with compost (if necessary), firm it lightly and evenly, and make sure it is thoroughly moistened by putting it in a shallow tray of water until the surface of the compost darkens completely, indicating that it has absorbed water all the way through. Then put the filled container to drain.

Finally sow the seeds thinly and evenly; in small pots or discs you should sow only two or three seeds in each. A dark airing-cupboard is a good place if you don't have a heated propagator to keep the pots or trays in until they germinate. Perennials can easily be grown from seed, though in many cases cuttings are quicker, and are certain to produce a new plant exactly like the parent.

The seedlings will take seven–fourteen days to germinate in most cases, though some may take weeks. Keep the compost moist and cover it with plastic sheet to help retain the moisture. If it becomes dry, the

Cut off a piece of rhizome (underground stem) with a leaf or two attached.

Plant the rhizome and leaves in a 7.5 cm (3 in) pot.

Fill almost to the top of the pot with compost, and firm down gently.

If the seeds are large enough to handle, space individually.

Smaller seeds should be sprinkled from their packets.

Protect with a piece of clear glass, or with plastic sheet.

seeds will not be able to continue germinating or even to start.

As soon as seedlings begin to appear, bring the containers out into a good light, and supply a slightly lower temperature. Turn them every day, otherwise they will grow too much towards the light. When they become large enough to handle, usually when the first true leaf appears, after the first two seed leaves, transplant them carefully with all their roots to 5-cm (2-in) diameter pots, one in each.

This is where the advantage of using small pots to start with becomes apparent, as the seedlings can be thinned to one in each, and left there until their roots fill the compost.

Make a hole in the centre of the compost in the pots with a pencil, and dig a seedling out of the tray with a plant label or the pencil, then lower it into the compost right up to its neck, so that the seed leaves are only just above the compost surface. This prevents it from having a weak main stem when adult.

Firm in the compost round it and water gently. If you are growing many varieties from seed, you can save space by transplanting the seedlings into a suitably-sized tray rather than individual pots; space the seedlings 5 cm (2 in) apart each way in this case.

Finally, put the newly transplanted seedlings in a little shade until they are visibly growing, and then move them into a good light. Remember that too much warmth will force the seedlings into growth too quickly and weaken them; it is better to keep the temperature in the low 60sF, or even less, if they are naturally cool-country plants.

Cuttings

Cuttings are pieces of stem which are put into moist compost and kept warm and humid from a few days to a few weeks, sometimes as long as a month or two. During this time they will develop roots from the cut end of the stem, and the stem itself will start to elongate, usually the first visible sign that rooting has occurred. The time to take cuttings is usually late spring until late summer.

Prepare a container by filling a 9-cm ($3\frac{1}{2}$ in) diameter pot with moist peat-based cuttings or potting compost, leaving a space at the top as usual. Using a pencil, make a hole in the compost at the side of the pot.

Then take a cutting, using the tip of a new shoot – you need a 10–13-cm (4–5-in) long piece, and should make the cut immediately above a leaf or pair of leaves. Then trim the cutting by removing a short length of stem just below a leaf, so that the cutting is now about 7.5–10 cm (3–4 in) long. Take off the lower leaves as well.

Put the cutting into the already prepared hole for up to two-thirds of its length, making sure that the base rests on the compost at the bottom of the hole. Then firm the compost around it, so that a gentle pull on a top leaf does not loosen it. Next, water lightly, and then insert two small pieces of split cane into the soil to keep a blown-up clear plastic bag away from the cutting. When the pot is inside this bag, secure it with a rubber band around the rim of the container.

Finally, put it in the shade, with a temperature of 18–21°C (65–70°F) until rooted; then pot each cutting separately.

The cuttings described above are called

soft cuttings or tip cuttings, and always consist of the end of a young stem which started to grow in the spring. They are used to increase many shrubs, trailing and climbing plants, and some herbaceous kinds such as busy lizzie. Most of these plants will be warm-country plants.

There are other kinds of stem cuttings which are also formed from young shoots of the current growing season, but these are more mature and are made later on in the year.

Half-ripe or semi-hardwood cuttings are taken in late summer and are generally longer, about 15 cm (6 in), made from side shoots rather than the tip of a main shoot. The cutting will have soft green skin on the stem at the tip, but at the other end the skin will have become almost hard and tough, and may be brown.

Hardwood cuttings are made in autumn, when the plants have finished growing for the season; the new season's shoots will have tough brown skin on the stems almost to the tip, and each cutting will be about 30 cm (12 in) long.

Both types of cutting will form roots at the cut end, as with the tip cuttings. They will probably take longer to do so, but need less warmth, and the hardwood kind are nearly always used for hardy shrubs. So for indoor plant increase tip or half-ripe cuttings are the kinds of most use.

As an insurance for rooting, there are special rooting powders available, into which the cut end of a cutting is dipped. These powders, which contain plant hormones, encourage the production of roots more quickly and make it more certain. *Air-layering.* A method of increase which uses a stem, but is really only a partial

In 2–3 months after air-layering a rubber plant, depending on the temperature, a number of roots will form from the cut.

stem cutting, is the kind called air-layering. You can do this to the rubber plant (*Ficus elastica* 'Decora') when it grows too tall, as it makes use of the top part of a stem.

The best time to do it is during early summer. Make a slanting cut in the stem about 30 cm (12 in) below the top and on the opposite side to a leaf-joint, so that the cut slants upwards towards the joint but does not go all the way through the stem. Put a match-stick in the cut to hold it open; it will ooze sticky white sap or latex, but this will be absorbed by the damp fibrous peat or sphagnum moss that you bind round the cut and stem. Tape a rectangle of clear plastic sheet round the stem above the cut and the peat and pull this down over the peat to contain it and form a sausage shape, then secure with more tape.

In two-three months, depending on the temperature, roots will form from the cut and be visible in the peat, and when there are plenty of them, you can cut the rooted top of the stem off completely, and pot it as a new plant.

Leaf cuttings. You can also make new plants from pieces of leaves. It sounds unlikely, but certain plants will also produce roots from leaves, provided they have been cut. Without getting too technical, a plant will often react to an injury such as a cut by producing roots, so that it can continue to live or continue the species with a new plant in the face of the threat to its existence produced by the cut.

Mother-in-law's tongue (*Sansevieria trifasciata* 'Laurentii') can be increased like this. Its stiff, upright fleshy leaves give the impression of stems, but nevertheless they are leaves, modified to their particular living conditions.

Chop a leaf into sections about 4–5 cm (1½–2 in) long, and stick them upright into peat-based cuttings compost so that they are half buried. Take care to place them so

Chop a sansevieria leaf into sections about 4–5 cm (1½–2 in) long, and stick them upright into peat-based cuttings compost.

that the cut edge nearest the base of the leaf is in the compost. Use a half-pot with drainage material in the base and space the cuttings about 4 cm (1½ in) apart; cover them with a clear, blown-up plastic bag secured round the rim, put in a warm place, 21°C (70°F) and rooting should occur within a few weeks. The summer is the best time for taking these cuttings.

The resultant plants will not, however, have the marginal yellow stripe of the parent plant; to obtain this, you will have to use division (see page 87), by cutting off

a piece of rhizome (underground stem) with a leaf attached, and plant that.

The Cape primrose (*Streptocarpus*) can be increased from leaves as well as by division. Again, cut a leaf into 5-cm (2-in) sections, and stick each upright into the compost, then treat them like the sansevieria, but plant them slantingly rather than upright, with a quarter of the leaf below the compost. For Rex begonias, make cuts across the main veins of a leaf, and then lay it flat on the compost, pinned down, or weighed down with small stones.

HOUSEPLANT FEATURES

NAME	HEIGHT	DIFFICULTY	MIN TEMP	LIGHT	HUMIDITY
Achimenes	30 cm (1 ft)	easy	7.5°C (45°F)	②	△△
Adiantum	23 cm (9 in)	less easy	4.5°C (40°F)	●	△△△△
Aechmea fasciata	38 cm (15 in)	easy	10°C (50°F)	①	△
Aglaonema	90 cm (3 ft)	less easy	16°C (60°F)	◐	△△
Ananas	38 cm (15 in)	less easy	10°C (50°F)	②	△
Anthurium	30–90 cm (1–3 ft)	difficult	16°C (60°F)	①	△△△△
Aphelandra squarrosa	45 cm (18 in)	less easy	13°C (55°F)	①	△△△
Araucaria heterophylla	1.8 m (6 ft)	easy	4.5°C (40°F)	◐	△△
Asparagus	60 cm (2 ft)	easy	10°C (50°F)	◐	△△
Aspidistra elatior	50 cm (20 in)	easy	4.5°C (40°F)	◐●	△
Asplenium nidus	45 cm (18 in)	less easy	16°C (60°F)	◐●	△△△
Begonia	15 cm–1.8 m (6 in–6 ft)	less easy	7.5°C (45°F)	①◐	△△
Beloperone guttata	45 cm (18 in)	easy	13°C (55°F)	②	△△
Billbergia nutans	30 cm (12 in)	easy	4.5°C (40°F)	●①	△
Bouvardia	60 cm (2 ft)	easy	10°C (50°F)	①	△△
Breynia	60 cm (2 ft)	less easy	13°C (55°F)	①	△△△
Browallia	45 cm (18 in)	easy	10°C (50°F)	②	△△
Calathea	38 cm (15 in)	difficult	16°C (60°F)	◐	△△△
Capsicum annuum	45 cm (18 in)	less easy	13°C (55°F)	②	△△△
Cephalocereus senilis	60 cm (2 ft)	easy	4.5°C (40°F)	③	△
Ceropegia woodii	90 cm (3 ft) trailing	easy	7.5°C (45°F)	②	△△
Chamaedorea elegans	1.2 m (4 ft)	easy	10°C (50°F)	①◐	△△
Chlorophytum comosum 'Variegatum'	30 cm (12 in)	easy	4.5°C (40°F)	①	△△
Chrysalidopsis lutescens	90 cm (3 ft)	easy	10°C (50°F)	①◐	△△
Cissus	1.8–2.4 m (6–8 ft)	easy	7.5°C (45°F)	●◐	△△
Citrofortunella mitis	60 cm (2 ft)	less easy	10°C (50°F)	②	△△
Clivia miniata	60 cm (2 ft)	less easy	4.5°C (40°F)	①	△△
Codiaeum	60 cm (2 ft)	difficult	16°C (60°F)	②	△△△
Coelogyne	30 cm (12 in)	easy	7.5°C (45°F)	①②	△△△△
Coleus	60 cm (2 ft)	easy	13°C (55°F)	②	△△
Cordyline	75 cm (2½ ft)	difficult	13°C (55°F)	①②	△△△
Cryptanthus	15 cm (6 in)	less easy	10°C (50°F)	①	△△
Cyanotis	15–23 cm (6–9 in)	easy	10°C (50°F)	②	△△
Cyclamen	30 cm (12 in)	less easy	4.5°C (40°F)	①◐	△△△
Cymbidium	60 cm (2 ft)	easy	7.5°C (45°F)	①②	△△△△
Cyperus	90 cm–1.8 m (3–6 ft)	easy	10°C (50°F)	①	△△△
Cyrtomium falcatum 'Rochfordianum'	30–45 cm (12–18 in)	easy	4.5°C (40°F)	①◐	△△
Dieffenbachia	1.8 m (6 ft)	difficult	16°C (60°F)	①	△△△
Dizygotheca elegantissima	1.2 m (4 ft)	difficult	16°C (60°F)	①	△△△
Dracaena	45 cm–1.5 m (18 in–5 ft)	less easy	13°C (55°F)	◐	△△△

LIGHT: good, lots of sun = ③   good, a little sun = ②   good, without sun = ①   light shade = ◐   shade = ●
HUMIDITY: some = △   more = △△   humid = △△△   very humid = △△△△

NAME	HEIGHT	DIFFICULTY	MIN TEMP	LIGHT	HUMIDITY
Dracaena surculosa	50 cm (2 ft)	less easy	13°C (55°F)	①	△
Epiphyllum	60–90 cm (2–3 ft)	easy	10°C (50°F)	①	△△
Epipremnum aureum	1.8 m (6 ft)	less easy	13°C (55°F)	①	△△△
Episcia cupreata	5 cm (2 in)	less easy	13°C (55°F)	①	△△△
Erica gracilis	45 cm (18 in)	less easy	7.5°C (45°F)	①	△△△
Euphorbia pulcherrima	45 cm (18 in)	less easy	16°C (60°F)	②	△△△
Exacum affine	23 cm (9 in)	easy	16°C (60°F)	②	△△△
× *Fatshedera lizei*	1.8 m (6 ft)	easy	4.5°C (40°F)	◑①	△△
Fatsia japonica	1.2 m (4 ft)	easy	4.5°C (40°F)	①◑	△△
Ficus benjamina	2.4 m (8 ft)	less easy	13°C (55°F)	①	△△△
Ficus diversifolia	60 cm (2 ft)	less easy	13°C (55°F)	①	△△△
Ficus elastica	2.4 m (8 ft)	easy	10°C (50°F)	①	△△
Ficus lyrata	1.2 m (4 ft)	less easy	10°C (50°F)	①	△△
Ficus pumila, F. radicans	45 cm (18 in) trailing	less easy	13°C (55°F)	●	△△△
Fittonia	10 cm (4 in) trailing	difficult	16°C (60°F)	●	△△△
Glechoma hederacea 'Variegata'	60 cm (2 ft) trailing	easy	4.5°C (40°F)	①	△△
Grevillea robusta	3 m (10 ft)	easy	4.5°C (40°F)	②	△△
Gymnocalycium mihanovichii 'Friedrichii'	7.5 cm (3 in)	less easy	13°C (55°F)	③	△
Gynura sarmentosa	60 cm–1.2 m (2–4 ft) trailing	easy	10°C (50°F)	②	△△
Hedera	90 cm (3 ft) trailing	easy	4.5°C (40°F)	①	△△△
Hedera canariensis 'Variegata'	1.2 m (4 ft) trailing	easy	10°C (50°F)	②	△△△
Heptapleurum arboricola	90 cm (3 ft)	easy	10°C (50°F)	①◑	△△
Hibiscus	90 cm (3 ft)	less easy	13°C (55°F)	②	△△△
Howea forsteriana	1.8 m (6 ft)	easy	10°C (50°F)	●	△△
Hoya carnosa	5 m (16 ft) climbing	easy	10°C (50°F)	①	△△
Hypocyrta glabra	25 cm (10 in)	easy	10°C (50°F)	①	△△
Hypoestes phyllostachya	30 cm (12 in)	easy	10°C (50°F)	②	△△
Impatiens	45 cm (18 in)	easy	16°C (60°F)	②	△△△
Jacobinia carnea	1.2 m (4 ft)	less easy	13°C (55°F)	①	△△△
Jasminum officinale grandiflora	5 m (16 ft) climbing	easy	4.5°C (40°F)	②	△△
Jasminum polyanthum	5 m (16 ft) climbing	less easy	7.5°C (45°F)	②	△△
Kalanchoe	15–38 cm (6–15 in)	easy	10°C (50°F)	②	△△
Lobivia	15 cm (6 in)	easy	0°C (32°F)	③	△
Mammillaria	2.5–15 cm (1–6 in)	easy	4.5°C (40°F)	③	△
Maranta	20 cm (8 in)	difficult	16°C (60°F)	①	△△△△
Monstera deliciosa	1.8 m (6 ft)	easy	10°C (50°F)	●	△△△
Musa	90 cm–1.2 cm (3–4 ft)	less easy	16°C (60°F)	②	△△△△
Neoregelia	20 cm (8 in)	less easy	16°C (60°F)	①	△
Nephrolepis	60 cm (2 ft)	easy	10°C (50°F)	●	△△
Nertera depressa	2.5 cm (1 in)	easy	4.5°C (40°F)	②	△△
Odontoglossum	45 cm (18 in)	easy	10°C (50°F)	①②	△△△△
Oliveranthus harmsii	45 cm (18 in)	easy	7.5°C (45°F)	②	△△
Oplismenus hirtellus 'Variegatus'	90 cm (3 ft)	easy	7.5°C (45°F)	①	△△

NAME	HEIGHT	DIFFICULTY	MIN TEMP	LIGHT	HUMIDITY
Opuntia	30–90 cm (1–3 ft)	easy	7.5°C (45°F)	③	△
Pachystachys lutea	45 cm (18 in)	less easy	13°C (55°F)	①	△△△
Pellaea rotundifolia	15 cm (6 in)	easy	4.5°C (40°F)	◐	△△
Peperomia argyreia	20 cm (8 in)	less easy	13°C (55°F)	①◐	△△
Peperomia caperata 'Variegata'	15–30 cm (6–12 in)	difficult	13°C (55°F)	◐	△△
Peperomia magnoliaefolia	30 cm (12 in)	less easy	13°C (55°F)	①	△△
Peperomia scandens 'Variegata'	60–90 cm (2–3 ft) trailing	less easy	13°C (55°F)	①	△△
Philodendron bipinnatifidum	1.2 m (4 ft)	easy	10°C (50°F)	①	△△△
Philodendron melanochryson	60–90 cm (2–3 ft)	difficult	16°F (60°F)	①	△△△
Philodendron scandens	2.4 m (8 ft) climbing	easy	10°C (50°F)	◐●	△△
Phoenix roebelinii	90 cm (3 ft)	easy	10°C (50°F)	◐	△△
Pilea cadierei	30 cm (12 in)	less easy	10°C (50°F)	①	△△
Platycerium bifurcatum	45 cm (18 in)	easy	10°C (50°F)	◐	△△△
Plectranthus oertendahlii	75 cm (2½ ft) trailing	easy	10°C (50°F)	①	△△
Pleione bulbocodioides	15 cm (6 in)	easy	4.5°C (40°F)	②	△△
Plumbago capensis	2.4 m (8 ft) climbing	easy	7.5°C (45°F)	②	△△
Pteris	30 cm (12 in)	less easy	10°C (50°F)	◐	△△△
Radermacheria	1.2 m (4 ft)	easy	13°C (55°F)	①	△
Rebutia	5 cm (2 in)	easy	7.5°C (45°F)	③	△–△△
Rhipsalidopsis gaertneri	23 cm (9 in)	easy	4.5°C (40°F)	②	△△
Rhoeo spathacea	38 cm (15 in)	less easy	10°C (50°F)	②	△△△
Rochea coccinea	38 cm (15 in)	easy	4.5°C (40°F)	②	△
Saintpaulia	15 cm (6 in)	less easy	16°C (60°F)	①	△△△
Sansevieria	15–60 cm (6 in–2 ft)	easy	10°C (50°F)	①	△△
Saxifraga stolonifera	30 cm (12 in)	easy	4.5°C (40°F)	①◐	△△
Schefflera actinophylla	1 m (3½ ft)	easy	13°C (55°F)	①◐	△△△
Schlumbergera × buckleyi	23 cm (9 in)	easy	13°C (55°F)	②	△△
Sedum sieboldii	23 cm (9 in)	easy	4.5°C (40°F)	②	△
Senecio macroglossus variegatus	1 m (3½ ft)	less easy	10°C (50°F)	②	△△
Setcreasea purpurea	90 cm (3 ft)	easy	10°C (50°F)	②	△△
Sinningia	38 cm (15 in)	less easy	10°C (50°F)	①	△△
Solanum capsicastrum	38 cm (15 in)	easy	10°C (50°F)	②	△△△
Sparmannia africana	90 cm (3 ft)	easy	7.5°C (45°F)	②	△△
Spathiphyllum	30 cm (12 in)	less easy	13°C (55°F)	①	△△△△
Streptocarpus	30 cm (12 in)	easy	4.5°C (40°F)	①	△△
Syngonium podophyllum	90 cm (3 ft)	difficult	16°C (60°F)	①	△△△
Thunbergia alata	1.5 m (5 ft)	easy	4.5°C (40°F)	①	△△△
Tillandsia	5–30 cm (2–12 in)	difficult	16°C (60°F)	①	△△△△
Tolmiea menziesii	15 cm (6 in)	easy	4.5°C (40°F)	①◐	△△
Trachycarpus fortunei	90 cm (3 ft)	easy	10°C (50°F)	①◐	△△△
Tradescantia	45 cm (18 in)	easy	7.5°C (45°F)	①	△△
Vriesea splendens	45 cm (18 in)	difficult	18°C (65°F)	①	△△△△
Yucca elephantipes	1.8 m (6 ft)	easy	4.5°C (40°F)	③	△△
Zebrina	60–75 cm (2–2½ ft)	easy	10°C (50°F)	③◐	△△

INDEX

INDEX

ACKNOWLEDGEMENTS

The Publishers wish to thank the following photographers and organizations for their kind permission to reproduce the following photographs in this book:
Eric Crichton 35, 89; Photos Horticultural 6, 39b; The Harry Smith Collection 22, 23, 26, 27, 34b, 36t, 37, 39t, 42, 43, 44t, 45b&t, 46, 47, 48b, 49, 50, 51, 53t&b, 56, 58t, 59, 60l, 61, 63b, 64, 65, 66b, 68, 73b, 74b, 75, 76, 90; Peter Stiles 34t, 69, 70, 71, 72, 73t, 74.

The following photographs were specially taken for the Octopus Publishing Group Picture Library:
Theo Bergstrom 11b, 20, 57t; W F Davidson 24t, 31, 33b, 67b; John Harris 9; Neil Holmes 21t, 48t, 63t; Melvin Grey 82; John Moss 66t; Roger Phillips 7, 8, 10, 12, 28, 32, 36, 38, 40, 41, 44b, 52, 55, 58b, 80; John Sims 19, 30, 78; Paul Williams 13; George Wright 25; Octopus 14, 24b, 29, 33, 54, 60r, 77, 86, 57b.